ABOUT THE AUTHOR

Sonia Ducie A.I.N., trained at the Connaissance School of Numerology in London. She has been practising Numerology for more than four years, teaches both business and personal workshops, and gives chart readings. She is also author of *The Self-Help Reflexology Handbook* (Vermilion).

To contact Sonia Ducie for charts, tapes and workshops, write to: Sonia Ducie c/o Thorsons, HarperCollins*Publishers*, 77–85 Fulham Palace Road, Hammersmith, London W6 8JB.

Please enclose a stamped, addressed envelope or international reply coupon.

IN THE SAME SERIES:

THORSONS
PRINCIPLES
OF

NUMEROLOGY

SONIA DUCIE

Thorsons
An Imprint of HarperCollins*Publishers*

Thank you to the Ducie family – Lilian, Catherine,
Michael, Barbara, Peter, Vivienne, Anna, Lara, Jeffrey
and Elizabeth, and also to Claudine Aegerter
and Teresa Chris.

Thorsons
An Imprint of HarperCollins*Publishers*
77–85 Fulham Palace Road,
Hammersmith, London W6 8JB

Published by Thorsons 1998
1 3 5 7 9 10 8 6 4 2

© Sonia Ducie 1998

Sonia Ducie asserts the moral right
to be identified as the author of this work

A catalogue record for this book
is available from the British Library

ISBN 0 7225 3580 5

Printed and bound in Great Britain by
Caledonian International Book Manufacturing Ltd, Glasgow

CONTENTS

INTRODUCTION

WHAT IS NUMEROLOGY?

Numerology is the psychology, philosophy and science of numbers. It can be described as a study of the mind – where each number offers you insights into your psychological patterns. It is also a philosophy – it offers you deeper meanings into the realms of existence. Numerology can also be described as a science, that can help you to solve certain problems or situations in your life or to explore your potential. Numbers influence your life in every way and Numerology can help you to understand more about life in general.

To practise Numerology you need to be able to add up simple numbers but you don't need to be a mathematician. Working out the numbers is only one part of Numerology, whilst using intuitive interpretation is another. Numerology is a method by which you can develop your intuition, as you learn to trust your response to the impression you get when you 'read' the numbers. When you have been working with numbers for a while you really get a feel for them and start to see the overall picture – the numbers talk to you!

In Numerology all life is governed by the numbers one to nine. Any number above nine can be added to form a single digit between one and nine. For example, if you are adding up the number 38, then 3 + 8 = 11, and 1 + 1 = 2, so the final number is two.

Numerology is applied to your date of birth and your names (particularly the ones on your birth certificate). Each letter equates to a number which when totalled gives additional information about your life. From A to Z these add up from 1 to 26. For example A = 1, P = 7, H = 8, etc.

Each number has many qualities, strengths and weaknesses, and negative and positive influences are associated with each cycle 1 to 9. Negative influences or qualities do not mean that something is bad, although it may seem like that. Negative qualities are weaknesses that are as important as your positive influences and strengths, because you can work on them to make them stronger. For example, if you have the influence of 4 in your chart, you may be lazy. You may regard this as a negative quality, but by being aware of it you can start to take actions (if you choose) rather than resisting life, and transform this quality into a strength.

You have a combination of positive and negative influences in your chart, and you use them to different degrees from day to day, and during different times of your life. For example, you may be a really positive person who makes the most out of your life. However, because of a current trauma you may display a majority of negative qualities or influences from the numbers in your chart for a time. Each number also highlights your potential within that cycle.

CYCLES AND TRENDS

All life evolves or changes at its own pace, and in its own time. The body breathes in (contracts) and breathes out (expands), trying to find balance (2) between both. Have you noticed when you are trying to plan a holiday, for instance, that whatever you do you simply cannot get away at that time? The flights are booked so you go 'standby' – but the flight gets cancelled! So you end up going a month later and it works out even better than it would have previously. This is because everything in life works out at its own pace and rhythm; you have your own personal rhythm or cycles too, as indicated by the numbers in your chart. Getting to know your own numerological cycles can help you find the best possible potential for all events and in all areas of your life.

From your Age Number you can see what current experiences may occur during that cycle. For example if you are aged 21 then you are in a three cycle (2 + 1 = 3); this means that qualities relating to a three will influence your life during your 21st year.

The first six years of any of your nine year cycles are related to physical experiences – you are out participating in life. Your seventh year is a year for bringing together the wisdom of the experiences in your previous six years. For example if you have worked very hard at studying for six years you may obtain your degree or certificate in your seventh year. Alternatively if you have been lazy and not studied hard enough you may fail your exam in your seventh year.

During your eighth year you reevaluate your previous seven years, and indeed every nine year cycle before that. Finally in your ninth year you are in a year of completing and beginning new ideas and situations. Often when you get to your eight and ninth year of your cycle, you may find there can be great changes in your life. This is because your body is renewing itself for a fresh cycle of one to nine, and working out what it needs to let go of, or take forward into the 1 to 9 year cycle phase. These changes may be emotional, mental, spiritual as well as physical.

PERSONAL INFLUENCE

Numbers influence every area of your personal life. From your date of birth, the types of experiences you will have are mapped out and fall into nine categories. However, how you use these experiences varies because everyone is unique. Even if you share the same date and exact time of birth as someone else (out of the current 160 people born every minute on planet earth), by the nature of the influences from your names (which are different) then you will experience life in your own way. Some people may experience the more positive aspects of their numbers rather than the negative, and vice versa, which produces differences even if your date of birth is the same.

How you experience your numbers also varies from day to day. Sometimes you may be really positive about life, and display many of the positive qualities in your chart, and on other days you may experience more of the negative energies attributed to your numbers.

Numerology can be easily used to observe past, present and future problems or situations. It is an inspirational tool that can help you to understand your psychological patterns. Therefore it can bring awareness to negative patterns which are keeping you stuck with recurring problems or unresolved situation, to help release them.

You can apply Numerology to find out more about your health. You can focus on your career. In order to highlight your talents and gifts, for example, to see whether it's best to be self-employed or work for a large or small company, or to see

when to leave or start a new job or career. You can explore compatibility within all kinds of relationships – with friends and family, with work colleagues and social acquaintances. In intimate relationships with a partner you can discover what core issues you are working on together, and the strengths and weaknesses within your relationship. Numerology can also focus on your finances, by highlighting natural cycles and potential times of abundance or scarcity. Numerology gives you great clarity about all areas of your life, and the world around you.

BUSINESS INFLUENCE

Names of your company and its birth date (that is your first day of trading) can be put into Numerological order to see its natural trends and cycles. For instance, if your company is in its third year of trading then one of the positive influences is that of expansion, or expanding on what you have already. You may do this by employing new staff, opening new offices, producing more products, etc. When your company is in its fourth year of trading, one influence is to consolidate your experiences (or what you've learned so far), consolidate resources, and to build a solid foundation within the company, etc. You can use Numerology in recruitment to see whether the job matches the person you are employing, both in character qualities, perseverance, and timing. If you are launching new products then Numerology highlights the maximum potential for the timing of the launch, the best possible product name, and even where to hold events (names and numbers of buildings are also important).

GLOBAL INFLUENCE

Your future depends on numbers literally – generating the energy by which you survive and grow. The most fundamental scientific representation of energy or life is the DNA code which has 46 combinations, that governs all humanity. Genetic engineering relies on these codes to identify illness (by numbers). Present and future generations are born out of the experiences inherited by previous generations which are all sorted in these genes or numbers. Indeed 46 adds up to a one, which is the number for new opportunities and an open book to all life experiences.

Money is counted in numbers, and has numerological value, which is a representation of energy. Modern life is dictated by computers (which use numbers), space age travel depends upon computers which are coded in to operate machinery. At the Olympics clocks have to be precision timed so as to assure the accuracy of each winner, etc.

Numbers are also added up to represent the important influences of the year you live in. For example 1998 adds up to nine, and this nine will influence all the experiences that the world has this year. One of the elements of the nine is power, and power can be used in a positive or negative manner. Nine is also a number which can bring environmental issues into the spotlight.

You can apply Numerology to unravel deeper meanings of historical events, to geography to find out why lands have changed and will change, to politics and economics, in a way to see the potential areas of strengths and weaknesses within each country and its leadership. It can also be applied to look at earth changes – volcanos, flooding, earthquakes – to highlight problem areas, and to timing when these events are most likely to occur. Numerology can be used to examine the field of medicine; by adding up the names or reference numbers allocated to each illness or medicine you can learn more about them.

WORLD EVENTS

You may think the world is a large place and what happens at the other side of the world has no effect upon you – but it does. For example, if there is a hurricane in one part of the world it causes a fluctuation in weather in the rest. Weather patterns can be studied by observing the appropriate year or date, which can help to explain why they occur.

By the same token world events affect everyone, and they can affect the trend for future events. For instance, can you remember a date which had a great effect upon your life? Maybe it was the day man first landed on the moon in 1969; astronaut Neil Armstrong said, 'One small step for man, one giant leap for mankind.' The year 1969 added up to a seven year and one of its qualities is the ability to bring things together. This one event affected the whole of space travel as it is today and changed man's perspective of the earth and moon forever.

Perhaps you remember the Live Aid concert on 13 July 1985. Were you touched and moved by the atmosphere (which was electric) or by compassion for the pictures of Ethiopian children on your television screen? That day 48 million pounds was raised. The day was the 13th, which in superstition is believed to be unlucky, but which actually is the number for transformation and change. The whole date adds up to a seven (again), and this event really did bring everything together and helped to materialize an abundance of money for Ethiopia and the children in need.

A major day in British politics was 1 May 1997 – Election Day – when after 18 years of Conservative government Tony Blair became the Labour Prime Minister. Eighteen adds up to a nine, and therefore Britain was discriminating about what to let go of, or to take forward, into its next nine-year cycle of politics. Nine is a number influencing endings and new beginnings.

By observing the Numerology of events which occur each day you can understand a lot more about the world in which you live, and how these events are affecting you.

LANGUAGES

Language is a method by which you identify your crowd, your community, group or family, and by which you communicate. All life is expressed through communication. Numerology is a universal language. All nations speak one language with Numerology, because every language can be translated into numbers and, therefore, can be understood. Languages that use symbols for letters, such as Japanese and Arabic, can also be translated into numbers by translating the symbols.

Music is also a language that can be deciphered numerologically to give meaning and depth to its hidden messages. Each note has a letter A to G, which adds up one to seven, with each flat and sharp adding finer tuning to each note by giving additional elements for that note to harmonize with the next. Each score is like reading a complete book which reveals a lot about

the composer's life, about the time in which it was written, and about what was truly being communicated.

Therefore, the simple language of numerology can help you feel connected to the rest of the world and realize that you are all sharing similar experiences in your own unique way.

A FINAL NOTE

You may think that all this information about life and Numerology is complicated but actually it is very simple because everything you need to know is contained in the numbers one to nine. Look to Chapter 1, 'Working Out Your Chart' to see just how simple it is to find out more about your own life by working out your own Numerology chart. You may even like to do charts for your friends and family too.

WORKING OUT
YOUR CHART

L earning to work out your own chart is easy once you
know how. At first you may only be able to understand
a little about the numbers but eventually it all slots
together. You would not work on a computer before mastering
the keyboard so remember that the more you know about each
number the more you get an overall picture of the chart. This
takes time but learning is great fun and it is fascinating to learn
more about each number. Learning Numerology is like learning to drive a car – you really try at first but once you are
relaxed you find your way around much more easily and take
in the whole scenery instead of just the road immediately
ahead of you.

YOUR KEY NUMBERS

The two most important numbers influencing your life are your
Personality Number and your Life Path Number, both taken
from your date of birth. Both these numbers portray strengths
and weaknesses, positive and negative attributes, and highlight your maximum potential in life.

Your personality Number reveals gifts and qualities which
are often very different from those associated with your Life

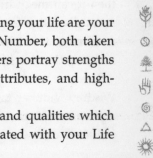

Path Number (unless both these two numbers are the same). Sometimes the qualities from your Personality Number are stronger influences over your life (at times) than your Life Path Number. At other times in your life your Life Path Number has a more powerful influence over your experiences.

When your Personality and Life Path Numbers are different, they can rub up against each other and cause a lot of conflict. It can literally feel as though there are two different people within you, each wanting something different. In an ideal world you are trying to find a way for your Personality and Life Path to meet so that you can gain the best possible experiences from both, and so they can live and work together in harmony. This is possible, and when these two numbers do work together you may find that your life flows over with positive experiences, and you can achieve great success in all areas of your life because you are fulfilling your maximum potential.

Sometimes your Personality Number and your Life Path Number are both the same. This means that the qualities, lessons or experiences identified with that number are stronger and more intense. For example, if both your Personality and Life Path Numbers add up to a 5, then you are a communicator or you need to work at communicating. This may mean (positively) with two fives that you may be brilliant in the field of communications, ie PR, marketing, travel, dancing. It is also a number indicating procrastination. So if you have two fives then it can mean (negatively) that you really need to impose some discipline to get things done. Five is also a number for freedom so if you have two fives then you may be very restless and skip through life, perhaps at times avoiding commitment.

The next most important influence in your life is from your Wisdom Number, taken from your full name, which gives you a practical gift to use in your life. Finally, your age is also an influence over the kind of experiences you will have during that year. Whilst your time of birth offers finer details about your life, it is not necessary for you to use this when you are working out a general reading for yourself or others.

YOUR PERSONALITY NUMBER

Your personality portrays characteristics which you were born with and inherited from your parents, and ones which you develop as life goes on. Your Personality Number is taken from the exact date in the month you were born. For instance if you were born on the 9th, then you have the influence from the 9 in your Personality. If you were born on the 25th you will have a 7 influencing your Personality ($2 + 5 = 7$) and so on.

LIFE PATH NUMBER

Your Life Path Number is the number for your direction or purpose in life; bringing awareness to this aspect can help you get clarity about your whole life, and give you a deeper meaning to your full potential. You find this number by adding up the whole of your date of birth. For example if you were born on 17th January 1969 then you would add $1 + 7 + 1 + 1 + 9 + 6 + 9 = 34$, $3 + 4 = 7$. So seven is your Life Path Number.

WISDOM NUMBER

The Wisdom Number highlights practical qualities or gifts you have or may accumulate, and can use in your lifetime. It is the wisdom of knowledge gained by experience which leads you to develop practical gifts which you can use to help yourself or even use them to help others. To work out this number you simply translate each letter into numbers (*see page 5*) and add together the whole name on your birth certificate. This includes any names registered including middle names. (If you do not have a birth certificate then go by the names first known to you.)

QUALITIES WITHIN YOUR NAME

You can take each of your individual names – Christian or first, middle, and surname or family name – and work out the number for each of them. The most important names are the ones on your birth certificate because these give you additional qualities, strengths and weaknesses which have a strong influence over your life.

When you look at all the numbers in your names notice if there are any that are repeated – you may have lots of 4s or 7s, for instance. This means that these are qualities you are strongly working with and which will influence you greatly. It can also mean that you are talented in the areas they refer to – if you have lots of 4s maybe you are a born organizer. Also notice what numbers are missing from your chart. These can indicate qualities you need to focus on to make you stronger, or they can be strong already, because you have been working with those qualities for a long time.

If your name has a prefix, ie MacClean, then include all the letters as part of the surname or family name. Similarly, double-barreled names or names like Van Der Holland, are generally considered to be all part of your surname. Names like Anne-Marie, Marie-Claire, Jean-Paul, are also considered to be one name, be it a first or middle name (but you can also add them up separately for fun to see what qualities each name brings on its own).

ALPHABET CHART

Here is a translation of the alphabet into numbers which you may like to study and memorize so that you can work out names and words quickly and easily. Numerology is easier to apply when you don't need to think too hard about how to 'work it out' because when you are relaxed it flows, and you enjoy it more.

1	2	3	4	5	6	7	8	9
A	B	C	D	E	F	G	H	I
J	K	L	M	N	O	P	Q	R
S	T	U	V	W	X	Y	Z	

YOUR AGE

Your age portrays an influence over each year it governs. It is worked out by simply adding your age to form a single number between one to nine. For example, if you are 27 then 9 (2 + 7 = 9) would be a current influence over your 27th year.

HOW TO WORK OUT A CHART
SOPHIE ANN GOOD, BORN 27.3.1981.

Here is an example of a typical chart which can help you to understand how to work out your own chart. Follow this carefully and you will sail through your own chart. Each number shows how the numbers may influence Sophie's life, and possible qualities that she may portray. Remember the two most important numbers in her life are her

Personality Number and Life Path Number, followed by her Wisdom Number, and her Age (for her current influences).

Sophie's Personality Number is 9 (this was found by adding $2 + 7 = 9$, because she was born on the 27th). Sophie has a caring and loving personality and is interested in helping others. She is very thoughtful and is interested in environmental issues, and education. She likes to treat people fairly and is very good at discriminating about situations and seeing both points of view. She is very powerful at getting her points of view across and often lectures people about her beliefs. Sophie is also very wilful and likes to get her own way. Although she is good at judging situations she also likes to think she is always right and she can be very stubborn. She is very critical of herself and others, and her high ideals can often lead her to frustration. She likes intellectual conversation and is very knowledgeable. Sophie is also a perfectionist and likes to dress well, although she can also be slovenly at times.

Sophie's Life Path Number is 4 (found by adding $2 + 7 + 3 + 1 + 9 + 8 + 1 = 31$, $3 + 1 = 4$, this number taken from her whole date of birth). Sophie is very practical, reliable, efficient and hard working, and is very good at organizing. She is a very reliable person and although she doesn't take to people straight away, once she knows them she can become a very loyal friend.

Sophie needs her security and having a career which she can stick to for life may be more interesting to her than swopping jobs every five minutes. Likewise a secure home base is very important to her and she needs to feel her long-term partner or mate will be loyal too. She likes to feel special and has a very real creative streak. She is resistant to change – she really does prefer to stick to the same things all the time and can be quite rigid. She prefers to dress practically and be comfortable most of the time rather than putting on a pair of shoes which will look nice, but will rub her feet. Sophie is very determined and has her feet firmly on the ground, and she is very responsible too.

Sophie's Wisdom Number is a 7; you work out this number by adding up the numbers for all the letters in her name:

1 6 7 8 9 5   1   5 5   7 6 6 4 = 70, 7 + 0 = 7

With a 7 Sophie's practical gifts are her ability to instigate things, to get things moving and to bring people together. She is brilliant at match-making, and also at materializing things. For example, if you need some-thing, chances are Sophie will know just where to find it. She just thinks something and it happens. (This isn't very good when she's in a bad mood because all kinds of things go wrong, for example, things fuse or the computer breaks down, and it's best to stay out of her way.) She is also prone to panic so if life gets too hectic she may 'throw a wobbly' (which helps her get out of doing things sometimes – very convenient). Sophie is very trustworthy and instils trust in others. She is also very intu-itive, and sensitive at times.

This year Sophie is 17 and she is in an 8 year (found by adding 1 + 7 = 8). Sophie is now reevaluating her last seven years of life – from the age of 10 to 16 – she is really changing. She is learning to stand on her own two feet, to find her own strength, and to assert herself in the world. Sophie has just become aware of the material world and really wants to be able to earn lots of money from whatever career she chooses. She can be manipulative and can sometimes be bossy and aggressive towards her friends and family. This year she is learning even more about responsibility.

OTHER INFLUENCES FROM HER NAMES

Sophie (167895 = 36, 3 + 6 = 9) adds up to 9. This is the same number as her Personality Number therefore the qualities of the 9 are stronger in her chart. She may eventually work as a teacher, but will focus on her own educational needs this year. She has an active mind, but can also be over-emotional at times. She needs to learn to let go and be more relaxed about life, particularly this year.

Ann (155 = 11, 1 + 1 = 2) is Sophie's middle name which adds up to 2. As a two Sophie can be very gentle with an ability to make decisions easily, and is able to weigh up situations; she is very observant. She is

caring and nurturing and can be cautious at times. Sophie is very good at lending an ear when her friends are upset and she would make a brilliant counsellor; she really listens to what you are saying. However, she can be very manipulative at times.

Her surname or family name Good is a 5 (7664 = 23, 2 + 3 = 5). Sophie's 5 influence means that she needs to learn to communicate and may be good at dancing. She loves adventure, travelling, and seems to have a zest for life. She is, however, rather unpredictable and has a habit of changing her mind about everything every two minutes.

THE OVERALL FEEL ABOUT SOPHIE'S CHART

Sophie's Personality Number is 9, her Life Path Number is 4, her Wisdom Number is 7, and her Age is an 8 (1 + 7).

Sophie has a strong mind, is very determined, and may be academic (or likes studying), and will certainly (in the positive) be able to materialize her goals. She has very high standards and ideals, and pays a great deal of attention to detail. She is very sensitive, and even over-sensitive and emotional at times, but with the influence of the 4 (Life Path) she is able to keep her feet firmly on the ground. She likes sports, and likes fairness in every area of life to be seen to be done. She would make a very good teacher, counsellor, carer, or humanitarian, but her ideal career may be in litigation – a judge, or even a politician who handles a great deal of power and authority.

She has a wicked sense of humour and can (unintentionally) be hurtful at times (influenced by her Wisdom Number 7). She may also have a gift with her hands and be very good at massage, and she may like to be physical with people she feels comfortable with.

Sophie can also be passive and may ruin wonderful plans with her overbearing leadership and her criticisms of herself and others. She is always judging people and may enjoy gossiping – in a playful way sometimes.

As she is in an 8 year she needs to learn to stand on her own two feet and reevaluate this year, and she may be cutting some ties with the past.

However, Sophie may also be restless and not brilliant at commitment, so she may change her mind many times before making any decisions ('Good' adds up to a 5). Next year she will be in a 9 year and ending her final year of this nine-year cycle.

SUMMING UP YOUR CHART – THE OVERALL PICTURE

Remember it takes time to get the overall picture about your life lessons or what strengths and weaknesses are influencing you. When you look at your chart first work out your Personality and Life Path Numbers, these are the two most important numbers. See how they work individually and how they work together. Perhaps try to observe which numbers have the most influence over your life at the moment.

Next work out your Wisdom Number and all other influencing elements including your age. It can be difficult to be objective about your own chart sometimes. You may like to ask a friend to help you with your chart, or have fun doing theirs.

Numerology is fascinating and reveals a lot when you piece each bit of the jigsaw together; it is the whole person that is important, not all the bits!

HISTORY

ZERO

Numerology was born out of the zero (0), which is the potential for all life; elemental life, vegetable life, animal life, and life in the human kingdom. All life is made up of energy, and energy is constantly changing and moving and creating more energy, or life.

The zero is often ignored in Numerology because people generally refer to the numbers one to nine. But the zero is essential and without it life could not exist. In Hebrew zero is the number for infinity, because zero is the number for all possible potential.

Numbers enabled mankind to produce the first understanding of life, how it was then, how it is now, and how it will be ... via the ability to interpret the cycles and trends and qualities contained within each number.

PLATO AND PYTHAGORAS

Plato was a philosopher and was responsible for recording much of the information about Numerology that he learned from Greek mathematician and philosopher Pythagoras. This was later passed down via its usage as a very simple and

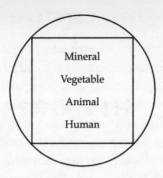

Mineral

Vegetable

Animal

Human

powerful system, which gives information about life via the numbers one to nine.

Pythagoras was one of the early Numerologists and masters. He taught his students to develop their intuition at his School of Mysteries in southern Italy around 600 BC. It is believed that he was a very strict man who paid great store by discipline, which was high on the agenda for his learned pupils. Pythagoras taught his students to use their intuition by learning about sound and music, arithmetic, astrology, and also focusing on colours. However, Pythagoras said that numbers were the 'essence of all life'.

It is possible that the religious teacher Buddha may have studied Numerology with Pythagoras and that these two masters may have worked together to relate the teachings which are still being interpreted today. It is likely he travelled to the East, particularly to India in search of his truth and knowledge.

OTHER SYSTEMS

There are many different systems or traditions in Numerology. These systems vary according to each country and the method employed. However, man has used his predicament and collective circumstances to interpret the numbers according to the world he has lived, and lives in, and according to his needs. For example, the early 'caveman' lived very much by his instincts. He needed to know where to track down his next meal, where to find a safe place to sleep, and about reproduction. Therefore counting animals – one dead animal may have lasted a whole family a week – would have been one of his most essential uses for Numerology. He worked very much at the physical level and as his needs were few, then on a daily basis he generally needed to count in fewer numbers.

Up to the middle of the 20th century many Numerologists paid great attention to the system 1 to 7, and 7 was the number for completion. People died much younger then. Generally the life expectancy for the masses was around 30(3) or 40(4) through disease or lack of sustenance. Many did not live to 70(7), 7, then, was a number for a priest, a spiritual healer, or a mystic who was 'special' and 'above the masses' in their ability to perform ritual magic, and with their claims to heal the sick.

People who followed Hebrew Numerology, often used the system of 1 to 12, as they saw 12 as a sacred and perfect number. This is because it is made up of 3 (with its religious meaning of holy trinity, and creativity), 4 (for the earth). They saw 7 as the number for completion or the full moon.

Now, with around 6 billion people on the planet, Humanity's needs have changed, and are constantly changing, which is reflected in the numbers we use. Today people have the luxury to be self-indulgent in the western world, and even in undeveloped countries live longer lives due to constant advancements in medicine. We have more choice now than our ancestors. There is more time to focus on desires and dreams and emotional well-being, rather than physical survival. This is reflected in Numerology which today recognizes the system based on 1 to 9, and 1 to 81(9), etc.

Numerology also recognizes 'Master Numbers' today, which are 11, 22, 33, 44, 55, 66, 77, 88 and 99. These intensify the lessons or influences from the individual number, and indicate extreme qualities or gifts which can be used to help others. For example, if you are a 66 you may work at serving your community through charity work or by taking on great amounts of responsibility such as being a diplomat, politician, serviceman, social worker, etc. Perhaps you may even be a great artist or musician reflecting life through your creative expression and by inspiring others.

Man has evolved, and lives in a world where there are no limitations on how many can be counted, particularly in the Stock Exchange, where billions of currency is counted every day. Computers use Binary code, zero and one, which was obviously no use to cavemen. Computers form their calculations using the Binary digits which are grouped into clusters of 8. So even computers have their own Numerology language!

CALENDARS AND DATES

Calendars are also a means to observe the consciousness of the world they mirror; but they do not all tell the same time or date around the world. For example, according to Western Time (the Julian or Gregorian Calendar), the year 1998 adds up to 9. In a 9 year man is discriminating about choices and is in a year of endings and new beginnings.

In Thailand the calendar indicates the year 2041 (adding up to 7). So this year they are learning to bring together the

wisdom from the experiences of the last six years. In Tibet the calendar year is 2125 (which adds up to 1); they are in a year of new beginnings, learning to forge ahead with new ideas and potential opportunities. The current Hindu year is 2055 (which adds up to 3); so they are in a year of expansion, and are learning more about self-expression. And so on.

These calendars are different because of changes made over the centuries, within each country, by their religious leaders or heads of state. For example, when there was a 'sacred birth' the calendar was sometimes changed to add an extra day to proclaim that 'special' event. In the sixteenth century Pope Gregory added ten days to the Gregorian calendar to bring it into line with the lunar and astronomical calendar at that time. Calendars were different because they were based on ancient methods of 'reading' time from the planets, the moon and the stars. The Babylonian calendar had 354 days in a year, instead of 365 in the Gregorian calendar, and these differences can be found amongst different civilizations around the world.

It is wonderful that many countries have their own calendars and dates, and it does not matter that they vary. They simply mirror each country or nation and its consciousness at that time. However, most countries use the Gregorian Calendar as their main point of reference, which is particularly essential in the world of business and economics.

In China in the past, many people did not reveal their correct date of birth from any calendar (and in modern times may register an incorrect date). It is said they believed Numerology to be so powerful that the Numerologist had the ability to 'extract their soul' by having the correct information. This is superstition but still exists in pockets today and can also be found in the West Indies, Africa and amongst many other cultures.

Sometimes when a Chinese person requests a Numerology chart it is transcribed with two dates of birth; one based on the

Chinese calendar and one on the Western calendar. Most attention is given to the date that is of most association and preference to the individual. Traditional Chinese people, it is said, still base their birthdate on the lunar months. Indeed when the Gregorian calendar says that they are 40, they may be 41 or older! Both charts offer information into the cycles and trends, and can be used together to draw key qualities influencing the life purpose, personality and potential, of the individual. This can also be applied to every other nationality which uses two different calendars.

METHODS OF INTERPRETATION

Many cultures use Numerology and their methods have been passed down for its modern interpretation and meanings by people of today. The Hindus use Numerology to impose beliefs and superstitions, and for prediction. Over the centuries their birth charts have been interpreted to reveal qualities and experiences for (particularly) the newborn child. It was (and still is to some extent) unthinkable for Hindus to have a child without consulting some mystic to predict its arrival or destiny in life. Often they used the method called Divination – or the calculation of numbers to predict an exact time or outcome of events. This method is still used today and is extremely accurate if used correctly and with discrimination. It is thought that the French 16th-century doctor and psychic Nostradamus was a Numerologist and most certainly incorporated this method in making predictions.

The ancient Tibetans also used methods of Divination which were employed by their Oracles (or mystics) who predicted the future, particularly for the State. It is said that the kings of Tibet relied heavily upon their information and made black and white decisions according to their statements.

China still has its book of insight or prediction and this is called the *I-Ching*, or the 'Book of Changes', which was written about 5,000 years ago, and is an ancient book of wisdom.

In Egypt, hieroglyphic symbols were translated into Numerology; an entirely unknown pictorial language giving the Numerologist detailed information into life at that time. These glyphs were used to veil certain revelations which have latterly been transcribed and understood. Numerology was also used statistically when the great mathematicians designed the Pyramids using numerological measurements in symmetry with the rays of the sun. These masters of numbers would spend time detailing their calculations and perfecting them to reveal one of the great mysteries of the world; how the extraordinary Pyramids were built.

It is said that Stonehenge was built around the time of the Great Pyramids. That is between 3000 and 1600 BC. These stones or monuments originally comprised of 56 circular wooden posts called Aubrey Holes. The 5 and 6 add up to 11, which is of course a master number, and one of its qualities is to inspire people with its creative and powerful energies. The 5 is for communication, the 6 is for wisdom and the 11 healing, so the people around at that time were magnetizing themselves with energy. Thousands of people from all over the world still visit the 54 stone monuments (which were later built and still stand) every year. Many more people visit the ancient Egyptian pyramids.

Another method of Numerology used to unravel information about past civilizations is via the use of symbols, and is called Sacred Geometry. Shapes like circles, squares, triangles, octograms, etc, are used to determine the number they represent within an area governed by a symbol. One example of this method would be in ancient Greece where it was used to count grain; by simply glancing at its shape, or geometry, it was easy to determine how much grain was available.

The Kabbalah is the Hebrew book based on the esoteric understanding of the bible, which uses the alphabet (and also the phonetic or sound alphabet) to find information about past, present and future for an individual from the names given at birth. These letters are transcribed into numbers and from that insights are given. They designate odd numbers as masculine and active, and even numbers as female and passive.

Finally there is the system called Esoteric Numerology, which is the study of concepts and abstract thoughts which material-ize into form or reality. It is said that 'energy follows thought' and that each thought creates the future, therefore thoughts are very powerful. This method of Numerology looks for the mean-ings behind the numbers, and the cycles and trends, strengths and weaknesses associated with each number. Looking behind numbers is very important; just because things aren't perceived does not mean that they do not exist.

It is said that human beings are only able to take in very little information at one time and when listening to a lecture (for example) only remember a fraction of the information. This is because the brain is busy assimilating each bit, and works like a computer digesting what it has learned, and cannot digest everything at once. Everything, therefore, boils down to inter-pretation, and a lot is missed out as a result of an individual's perception. So people generally see the black and white but it is the grey area that is sought in Esoteric Numerology.

Mind

Body

Spirit

MODERN DEVELOPMENTS

Many Astrologers and Tarot readers today also employ Numerology with their tools; indeed all these methods co-exist and are connected with each other as methods to interpret life.

Numerology is constantly changing and adapting to the society and world it mirrors. As man edges into the 21st century, the 'Age of Aquarius', new qualities will emerge for each number. For example, a 7 in the old days was a mystic, in the 1990s a 7 is a great materializer and an instigator, and in the year 2009 perhaps the 7 will be viewed as a revealer of new ways of working? Master Numbers may be more pronounced in the next century with more and more people working for their community and the world at large.

The year 2000 adds up to a 2, and the whole of the next millennium is a time to learn about sharing, co-operation, balance, and choice. Perhaps inner peace – another quality of the number 2 – can be achieved by living in harmony with the earth and its peoples by the end of the third millennium. Who knows!

Birth

Death

Rebirth

NUMBERS AND LIFE EVOLVE

Numbers are constantly changing or evolving and each generation projects its own interpretation upon these numbers. What you are told today about Numerology mirrors the experiences right now in the world. But in 20 or 200 years time some of this information will be outdated and largely incorrect. This doesn't mean Numerology is wrong, it just means that it is constantly adapting to its environment or the consciousness of the people who use it at any time. Therefore, the best way to get the most out of Numerology is to use it in the present – right now – and enjoy every moment. Have fun!

3

NAMES

WHAT IS IN A NAME?

Names are very influential because their Numerological qualities (both positive and negative) sum up what they are really trying to communicate. Have you ever thought, 'I really like that name' – that is because its qualities make you feel good, and resonate with a part of yourself that you like. You can also dislike a name in the same way, meaning you dislike qualities it gives. Similarly, you can feel completely indifferent about a name, maybe because you do not identify with the qualities it contains, or you may feel completely comfortable about them.

Names reveal numerological qualities which you may be unaware of; therefore studying Numerology can help you to understand what messages you are giving out when you use these names. Names are something by which others identify you, products, buildings, places, and so on.

You also associate positive or negative qualities with names that you have come into contact with before. For example, if you like the name Laura, it may be because of its association. Perhaps Laura was your boss who gave you promotion and a salary raise. By adding this name up you can find out why; Laura adds up to 17/8. Maybe there are qualities (therefore numbers) in this name that you identify with? Laura was empowering you with authority (qualities of the 8) by giving you promotion. She was also rewarding you with extra finances (8 is particularly connected with money and materialism). You may even find out that you have a number of 8s in your Numerology chart.

You associate feelings with names. A brand of toothpaste may add up to the same number as your partner's name, 5 for instance. With your partner you feel magnetic, sexual and adventurous. Therefore every time you use the toothpaste you are influenced by the good feeling you have about your partner!

YOUR BIRTH CERTIFICATE

In your Numerology chart your date of birth contains the most important influences over your life, followed next in importance by the names on your birth certificate. These names which are given to you at birth reveal finer details about your identity, your potential, and practical gifts you may have. They can be 'read' to extract more information about your strengths and weaknesses, and indicate more about the types of experiences you may have during your lifetime.

If you do not have a birth certificate (which still happens in some countries around the world), then simply take the names that were first known to you, including your middle names.

Parents have usually chosen your birth names. It is fascinating to discover whether there was an indecision about what your names should be. For example, perhaps your mother wanted to call you one name and your father another. Try adding up other names that may have been given to you, to see what qualities your parents were trying to give you within your names on your birth certificate. You can also note whether either of them wanted your names to be spelt differently to

what they are now, and to also add these up to see the strengths and weakness and potential they were trying to give you.

ADOPTION NAMES

If you know your full names according to your birth certificate, then use these as the most accurate influence over your life. They may even help you to understand why you were adopted. However, if you have (from a very early age) always used your adopted names, and you do not wish to associate with your birth names, then use these as the guiding influence over your life. Sometimes your full adopted names contain aspects of your birth names anyway. If you do not know your birth names then take your adopted names to reveal your strengths and weaknesses and your potential.

MARRIED NAME

Your married name (add up your first, middle names and sur-name) brings extra qualities that you are learning about from your partner, but do not replace the influence of the names on your birth certificate. You may find that married names, or their numerological meanings, also pop up in other areas of your chart. For example, if your birth month is the 7th or July then you may find your married name adds up to 7. If this is so then it is showing you some experiences or qualities that you need to develop or work with in your life. Also it shows your partner what strengths you are bringing to that relationship.

Your full married name also shows you potential problem areas or weaknesses that you have inherited by taking on the marriage name, which you can then strengthen. Weaknesses are as important as strengths, because you know your strengths, but a weakness or pattern transformed makes you grow, and feel stronger within yourself. For instance, you may have inherited a 4, and with a four you can be impractical, so through your partnership with your husband you may learn to become more practical!

Sometimes, a woman may decide not to take on her husband's name after she marries but keeps her maiden name. This can mean that she prefers to keep her own identity and independence (maybe she has a 1 in her chart). Alternatively, it may be that she is resisting fully entering the marriage union. But this is a choice, and particularly where the woman is working in the business field, she may like to keep using her own name which suits her working environment, and her business identity.

'PET' NAMES OR PSEUDONYMS

Pet names are usually given to people as a sign of affection. They can be used between friends, between a mother and a child, or in an intimate relationship, between lovers for instance – to imply a special 'bond' or connection between the two. Lovers' names may only be used in private, for bedtime between the bedsheets, or during intimate telephone conversations (or if you are very extrovert in public!) You may call your favourite aunt 'sweetie pie' because she is always baking you cakes.

Michael Jackson adds up to 7, for someone who is a creative materializer. He is often portrayed as a 'larger than life character', particularly in his breathtaking stage sets and videos. However, one of the 'pet' names given to him by the public is 'Jacko' which adds up to a 4, revealing people's views of him as being hard-working and determined.

'Pet' names highlight qualities that the other person sees within you, and identifies with; these numbers may also be present in their chart. However, they also may be qualities that they would like you to have ... have you noticed that when you are

having an argument with someone you are close to, you may call them by another name? For instance, if your friend Annabel likes to be called Bella, in an argument you may call her by her full name, just to annoy her! Annabel adds up to a 4, which describes a person who can be very serious, and Bella adds up to 5, which can be light and communicative. You can see why, in an argument when you want to be taken seriously, you would use Bella's full name!

Work out some of the numerological qualities for 'pet' names that you give people, and they give you. See what these names are teaching you about yourself and your life. For instance, if you would like your partner to be more adventurous then you may give them a 5 … if you'd like them to be more patient you may give them a 7 or an 8, or a 4 to be more practical, etc.

CHOOSING CHILDREN'S NAMES

Numerologists often get asked to help find the most suitable names for newborns; they simply look to the parents' charts for guidance. This is because a child carries the genes or chromosones from its mother and father, therefore it is natural that it also takes numbers from its mother's and its father's chart too. Numerologists do not choose the names for the child as such, but indicate its potential based on the parents' charts, or from the date of birth. Parents usually present a number of names (that they will have instinctively associated with the child) and the Numerologist gives some indication to their numerological meaning. You can also work out the numbers yourself to help you choose a name for your child, and follow your instincts about the 'right' one … as parents you know best!

STAGE NAMES

A stage name is a name taken on by an individual to use within the media so as not to reveal the birth or personal names. Elton John is a stage name. He was actually born Reg Dwight. The stage name is very important because it actually portrays what the person is projecting and what qualities they are working with, in the public eye. Influences from these names can be very powerful. Stage names often reveal qualities that the person needs in order to help them carry out their role on life's stage; on the television screen, on the radio, and in newspapers and magazines.

Mother Teresa was a stage name and adds up to 66 (3). She was someone who was devoted to her work in charity and who used her hands as a form of expression.

NAMING BUSINESSES AND PRODUCTS

If you are a retailer selling beauty products then you need the number for beauty and aesthetics to be reflected in the name of your products, your shop name, and in connection with any communications campaign associated with it. You may have a company which is very successful, and all the products sell abundantly, except for one line. This may be because of its name or the timing of its launch. Your company name also mirrors the vision of the people in it. So ideally, a dance school whose main theme is education needs 9s in its name (for education) as well as 5s (for dance), for example.

CHANGING NAMES

Have you ever thought of changing your names so that you can create a new identity? What is wrong with your current one?

What experiences are you trying to avoid? If you think you will change your name because it will … bring you more money, make you more attractive, etc, then think again. If these are not your personal numbers then they do not have integrity with who you are. Perhaps your middle name belonged to your grandparent, and you don't like that association because he or she had qualities you dislike. Perhaps your name adds up to the same as your parents and you simply cannot live up to their expectations, and so on.

Your names are your personal gifts and it is up to you to make the most out of what you have been given; after all, you are unique! Maybe you can acknowledge all your positive qualities, gifts, and strengths, and work towards fulfilling your maximum potential. It can also help when things are going wrong to learn to be patient with yourself, and learn to love and accept yourself as you are today.

VARIATIONS ON YOUR NAME

You may like to use variations of your birth name within different situations and with different groups of people in your life. For example, if your name is Jacqueline Mary Robinson (which adds up to an 8), then that is the name known to your family. As a lecturer at work you may like to be called Jacqueline M Robinson (adds up to 9), and to your friends you may be known as simply Jacquie (3) or even JR (1).

Some people 'ignore' their first name and use their middle name because they prefer it; this may be because the first name is a relative's name or because it feels uncomfortable to use. Look up the meaning for your first name and see what qualities you dislike about it, and what positive potential it holds for you.

All these variations help you to explore different qualities available to you from your full names on your birth certificate.

You may find that after using variations for a short time you decide to go back to your full name because you have explored enough!

LIKE ATTRACTS LIKE

Do you always find that you keep attracting people with the same name, or names that add up to the same number? Chloe had a boyfriend whose name and date of birth both added up to a 2. She discovered that her new boss's name was also a 2. This is no coincidence, but synchronicity, because Chloe's date of birth is a 2, so you can understand why she keeps attracting this number, because she is strongly identifying with its qualities.

Alternatively, Chloe may have an 8 missing from her chart (that is, there are no 8s in her full names from her birth certificate). So she attracts a partner who has an 8, or lots of them, so that she can learn about the qualities, strengths and weaknesses of this number. This also works both ways; if Chloe's partner has a 3 (for example) missing from his chart, he may need to learn about the qualities of the 3 in Chloe's chart.

You can apply numerology to all the names in your chart – your first name, middle names, and family name, and then look up the meanings of the appropriate numbers in Chapter 5. Some of the numbers you may identify with and others you may not, but they are all parts which make up the whole. You can also work out your friends', family's and partner's numbers to reveal just what numbers you are attracting.

MAKING THE MOST OF YOUR NAMES

Whatever your names are you can make the most out of the opportunities they offer you by building on your strengths, and learning more about your weaknesses you can improve upon them.

PLAYING WITH NUMBERS

Numbers influence everyone. You are given a date of birth, you count each day, you count money, you live by the clock – time. From telephones to faxes, computers to long distance running, all life is made up of NUMBERS!

You may be surprised about just how much information you can discover about your environment by applying the simple tool of Numerology. Discovering new things about life stimulates you; new things give you new energy which also helps to energize others. Numbers spring to life when they reveal qualities contained within them.

Next time you take a walk through your local neighbourhood, notice names on advertisements and add them up to see what messages they are giving out to the world. Work out the name of your boss, your colleagues at work, your friends and family, and work out their dates of birth if you like. Look at newspaper boards, their headlines, and the dates things occur and note the issues involved. For example, the headline for the 8th of the month may concern finance, and money is associated with an 8. Observe names of famous people on television and the type of programmes they are participating in or presenting. Are they the best type of person for the job, what qualities do their names project?

When you go shopping, note the brand names for your purchases, add them up and perhaps you can learn why you prefer one brand over another. What qualities do you like or dislike about a product brand? You can explore other areas; what are your favourite foods, flowers, music, etc. Do you like tennis (9), swimming (8), skiing (6) or golf (4)?

What names have you given to your pets? Fifi (3)? Oscar (2)? Lucy (7)? Pooch (3)? Add these names up and see from their personality and temperament if you have given them suitable and helpful names. What type of pets do you have: a cat (6), a dog (8), a rabbit (7), a horse (2), or a pet snake (5)? Look up these numbers in Chapter 5 and learn more about what it is telling you about them and you!

Once you open up to numbers they jump out at you from every angle and you can really have fun! It's fascinating – opening up to a whole new world of information and insights.

A DAY IN YOUR LIFE

Every day of the week has a number – Monday is the first day in each week when everyone experiences a mini new beginning or fresh start. Tuesday is the second day of the week, a day to try to find balance in your life, and so on. Each day everyone is influenced by the number for that day and this is called a 'general trend'. Another 'general trend' is the yearly trend which affects everyone (for example 1998 adds up to nine; this number influences everyone's life during this year).

You may like to add up each word, for each day, e.g. Wednesday (36 = 3 + 6 = 9), but different languages will yield different numbers, which can be complicated. It is much more simple to number each day of the week consecutively, 1 to 7, which is recognized worldwide.

NUMBER	DAY	INFLUENCE
1	Monday	beginning
2	Tuesday	balance
3	Wednesday	self expression
4	Thursday	work, creativity
5	Friday	movement, travel, sex
6	Saturday	relationship, family, sex
7	Sunday	rest, vacation

When you wake up in the morning, what time does your clock say? What number does the time add up to? Perhaps it's an 8 for responsibility. You make food, what's the number for food? That is a 3 for creativity and expansion. Then you go to work – 4, for discipline and structure. On your way to school (9 for education and learning) or university (1 for new intellectual stimulation and opportunities), the sun is shining. The sun adds up to a 9 for power. At work you have fun – 5 for adventure and stimulation. You go to the shop and spend some money which also adds up to 9 for power. Then you may return home to your Mr (4 for earthiness), Mrs (5 for communicative) or Miss (6 for wholeness) and your family (3 for expansion). You may have sex which adds up to a 3 for self-expression, family and creativity. (Note food and sex are both 3s!!!)

YOUR PERSONAL CREDENTIALS

Make up a personal Fact File to discover more information about your life by applying Numerology. Each entry will add up to a number; this number is an influence on the appropriate area of your life it refers to. For example, if your passport number adds up to 1 then this number can influence your experiences during the life of that passport. So with a 1, you may be seeking to explore new areas in life; you may like to travel to

unusual places or invent a holiday yourself, or travel may be your ambition. If you use your passport for work travel then the number 1 may throw up lots of opportunities – one of the qualities of the 1, etc.

LUCKY NUMBERS

Every number has the potential to be lucky because each number has its own positive trends and negative ones too. However, you may find in your life that certain numbers recur, and if these numbers bring happy events then you may suppose them to be Lucky Numbers for you. It is a popular belief that your birth date (i.e. your Personality Number, or your Life Path Number), gives you your lucky numbers, so for many this is so.

However, numbers also become lucky if you think they are because you give them an abundance of positive energy, which can attract a positive response.

FATE NUMBERS

Fate numbers work in the same way as Lucky Numbers but are eventful and you may not regard the events associated with them as being good or bad, but simply times of change. For example, some important event always happens to Philippe on the 12th of the month, at 12 o'clock, or in Flat 12, and December (12) is a big month for him. Twelve is therefore Philippe's 'fate' number. Maybe Philippe was born on the 12th!

LEARNING IS FUN

Learning about life by looking at all the numbers around you, and understanding the importance of their influences, can help you to go deeply into life and enjoy its full potential. The

importance of these numbers is reflected at home, at work, on the street, by your pets, in the weather, and in every walk of life. Enjoy Numerology and let it teach you more about yourself and the world you live in.

5

INTRODUCTION TO THE NUMBERS 1 TO 9

The following chapter explains many qualities and meanings of the numbers one to nine, and indicates ways in which these numbers can influence your life. When you work out a number, you must remember that you are not that number, but that the number influences you. For example, you may have a 5 Personality Number. This means the 5 influences your Personality, not that you are a 5!

WORKING OUT YOUR CHART

When you are working out your chart it is a good idea to focus on only one area at a time. For example, work out your Personality Number and learn about that, before moving on and finding out about your Life Path Number. When you are very familiar with these two numbers you can feel how they relate to each other, and how they influence your life. You can also look up the key qualities from your Personality and Life Path numbers together in the section at the end of each Number 1 to 9.

Next look at your name and work out your Wisdom Number. Then work out the influences of your Age on your current year's experiences. You may also like to add up your individual names to see their strengths and weaknesses and potential too.

Write all your numbers down on a piece of paper, and gradually, as you start reading about these numbers, try to get a feel for the overall picture. For example, are you very organized and methodical (strengths), or unfocused and rigid (weaknesses)? The overall picture may be that one helps to balance the other one out.

Look at the positive and negative qualities which influence each number. Sometimes you can experience the negative influences from your number, and at other times more of the positive influences. However, you experience a mixture of both to different degrees and at different times.

From the numbers you may recognize a pattern of behaviour, and you can learn about yourself. You may see things that you may like to improve upon, if you choose, and areas of potential. For example, with a number 2, you may make a good counsellor. Perhaps you are not brilliant at listening to people. So, if you would like to become a counsellor you can start by being aware of people when they are talking, or taking a professional counselling course.

VARIATIONS

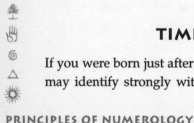

Sometimes you can see from your chart that you use more of your Personality Number than your Life Path Number and vice versa. Therefore the dominant number can have a stronger influence over your experiences in life. Becoming more aware of the strongest numbers that influence you can help you to get the most out of your life, and to fully experience each day's potential.

TIME OF BIRTH

If you were born just after midnight then it is possible that you may identify strongly with the qualities from the day before.

For instance, if you were born on the 14th at 11.45 pm, then the Number 15 may be more accurate when describing your personality. Therefore look up the following day's number to see if this is so for you. If you were born on the 15th at 1am, then you may be influenced by the 14, so look up this number too.

FAMOUS NAMES

At the start of each number section there are the names of some famous people who may share the same number as you (these dates of birth have been published in the media, and are correct as far as is known). It is interesting to see what qualities these people project to the world, as they go about their lives in the public eye.

COUNTRIES

What countries attract you, or would you like to visit? These countries may share the same number that is in your chart, or carry a similar vibration of energy. When you visit a country that you identify with it can help you with your personal development and growth, and can expand your knowledge about the world you live in.

CHARTS FOR YOUR FRIENDS AND FAMILY

It is great fun to work out a chart with a friend or member of your family, and to let them 'read' your chart too. This can help you both to learn more about each other and to develop your intuition as you learn to trust what the numbers are revealing about your life.

PRINCIPLES OF NUMEROLOGY

NUMBER 1

FAMOUS ONES

Diana, Princess of Wales, Sophia Loren, Jack Nicholson, Tom Wolfe.

COUNTRIES

Israel, Turkey, Egypt, India, Pakistan, Afghanistan, Caribbean.

GENERAL MEANINGS

One is the number for new beginnings, new life, new ways of doing things, new opportunities, new goals, and it is also the number for destruction (for breaking down old patterns, or old ways of doing things).

PERSONALITY NUMBER 1

POSITIVE

With a 1 influencing your Personality you are highly creative with a driving ambition towards your goals, whether they be in your personal or professional life. You see life as a challenge and staying focused on your goal makes the ride enjoyable. With a 1, the emphasis is not so much on achieving your goals (although you do like it when you do) as about the process by which you get there. It is the actual focus and creativity which excites you. You need challenges, either large or small, and tend to take them in your stride.

You are a creative ideas person, and are able to bring 'out of the hat' completely new ideas, and execute them in your own unique way. You are dynamic and highly charged with creativity. You exude energy and vitality and have staying power to go for what you want, with a get up and go that makes you strive for more.

You enjoy intellectual stimulation and enjoy learning; you need mental and physical challenges. A game of chess, a book or a good crossword may appeal, as much as an aerobics class, or a good workout. Exercise helps you to release any excess energy, particularly at the end of a day.

With a 1 you can also be compulsive about life, and do things just for the sake of it. For example, each morning you go out for a jog and you really enjoy it. However, after six months your interest goes, but you keep on jogging, not because you want to, but simply out of the compulsive drive to keep going. Equally, you are good at finding new things to do to stimulate your body and mind.

If you have a 1 influencing your Personality you can also be a pioneer, who loves to climb mountains or to explore virgin territory, where you can be stimulated by new life and discover new things.

With a 1, you are a strong individual and you often feel the need to find your own sense of individuality, like a wine with a unique flavour. This may show itself in the way you dress, the work you do, or the way you speak. You also enjoy your own company, and love to do things on your own, at times.

NEGATIVE

With the 1 influencing your Personality you are a detached person, and you may fear any kind of intimacy. You can also get 'stuck' emotionally, and be unable or unwilling to relate to people. You may prefer to work on your own, where you can remain uninvolved with others. Here you can focus on your goals unimpeded by the emotions of people around you, which you can find difficult to handle. Alternatively, you can also get carried away with your goals, and get too involved with work or with people at times.

You can be extremely self-centred and see everybody's lives through your own eyes and only relate to situations by how they may affect you. 'Me, me, me', is what matters and no one else exists. You are very good at looking after number one. With a 1 you may not care for what others think or feel and disregard them altogether; they are not important, but only what you feel and think matters.

Your ability to focus can also be a problem when you get stuck on one thing and refuse to budge. This can be at work or within a relationship. Then others try to drag you out of a rut, rescue you, or dig you out, which can be very exhausting for them and more difficult when you refuse to move. In fact, the harder people try, the more you may insist on digging your heels in.

With a 1 influencing your Personality you can also be withdrawn, lonely and self-pitying. You can be fearful about not being able to achieve your goals, which in itself can hold you back from trying. Alternatively, you can also be overpowering in your drive for your goals, and you may 'walk all over people', whom you think are holding you back.

Sometimes, you may lose the enjoyment, or enthusiasm, of working towards a specific goal, and your creativity and ideas may dry up. For example, you may have spent two years working on a new invention, a product, which could be sold all over the world. However, after all your hard work and focus, the invention doesn't sell. You may not feel like going for any other goals, or inventing anything else, for a while.

You can also reject other people's ideas or suggestions as invalid, and may not accept their way of living.

Perhaps you may also have a head full of so many inventions and new ideas, that you almost 'blow a fuse'. You just cannot get your creative force out of you fast enough, but you cannot do everything at once! At these times you can become destructive, because you may lose your focus and your concentration. Then your energy may not be channelled into your creativity but disperse into thin air.

With a 1 influencing your Personality you may be lacking in your own individuality, and you may like to have others around you who are strong individuals. You can also feel challenged and threatened at times, when others assert their own individuality.

LIFE PATH NUMBER 1

POSITIVE

If your Life Path Number is influenced by a 1, you are learning to work towards your independence. You are very directional, and know where you are going from one moment to the next in your life. You are a born leader.

NEGATIVE

You may want to be led instead of taking the lead. You may be dependent, lost without direction or drive and want others to do things for you. You may be dictatorial and use your leadership in selfish ways that are only to your advantage.

WISDOM NUMBER 1

POSITIVE

If a 1 is influencing your Wisdom Number, then you are able to bring in your practical gifts of courage when breaking down old ways of doing things, and courage to face new life. The number

1 is associated with your 'will', and the strength of will to carry things forward on your own, and as an independent person. You have an ability to overcome obstacles and like to include everyone in your life and treat everybody equally.

NEGATIVE

You may be arrogant and exclude others, believing yourself to be superior. You may enjoy being destructive and use this power for your own ends. You may withdraw as your line of defence.

HOW THE NUMBER 1 INFLUENCES YOUR:

HEALTH

You enjoy physical exercise – working out in the gym, aerobics, jogging – to help keep you fit and mentally alert, although at times you can become overfocused and preoccupied with this too. You enjoy the challenge of working out because it is another goal that you can achieve each time you do it. During certain periods of your life you may resist exercise as you remain focused solely on other things, or you just 'can't be bothered to make the time'.

You may be the type of person who doesn't like making a fuss about your health problems, and only visit your doctor, dentist, chiropodist, therapist, etc, when you think it is very important. 'If I must go' are words you may utter. This is also because any time taken away from your creativity (at home or in the work place) seems an unimaginable distraction.

However, you always seek out the best opinion when you seek help for your health and will rely on finding people who are leaders in their field. You listen to the professionals' opinions, and generally follow through with sensible advice to the

'T'. However, you are headstrong, and can at times prefer to do your own thing anyway, and remain single-minded in your outlook when it comes to your own health.

RELATIONSHIPS

You are striving towards independence, therefore you may attract partners who are also independent, or a dependent partner who can teach you about involvement. You may go for a long time without getting deeply involved within a relationship. Maybe because you choose to focus on other areas in your life, or because you fear involvement and emotions, or because you are afraid of intimacy. However, it may be helpful for you to get deeply involved within a relationship, to learn about attachment and intimacy, and to learn to 'open up'.

Involvement means thinking and caring about your partner and not just yourself, and with a 1, this can be difficult for you, because you are a self-centred person at times.

Once you are willing to go for a relationship, you are prepared to put in all the effort, energy and focus to help make it work. You are a strong individual, and will take problems within the relationship as challenges and tackle them head on.

If you are unfocused and lacking in creativity for a time in your life, and do not feel like you are achieving anything with your partner, there may be frustration which leads to an over-expression or outbursts of suppressed emotion.

CAREER

You are a born leader and so may be a leader in politics, fashion, art, music, in fact a leader in any field. With a 1 influencing your career, you are also good at taking over or running things – companies, projects, etc. You can inject enormous amounts of energy and vitality into whatever you choose to focus upon.

You may be an inventor, or a brilliant designer, or a creative ideas person whom your team relies upon for originality and flair.

FINANCE

Learn to focus on your gifts of creativity because your dynamic energy can help to bring in dynamic amounts of money too! However, money is not your main concern – you work because you enjoy working towards goals and being creative and you would even work for very little, because you love what you do. With a 1 you may not necessarily be 'good' at handling money because it isn't the most important thing in your life.

HOW YOUR PERSONALITY AND LIFE PATH WORK TOGETHER

If your Life Path Number is a 1, look below and match it up to your Personality Number; these two numbers offer the strongest and most important influences over your life. Read a few key points about how your Personality and Life Path Numbers work together.

1 LIFE PATH WITH A 1 PERSONALITY

If both your Life Path and Personality Numbers are 1 then this intensifies the influences of these qualities. You may be extremely focused, ambitious with a flair for goal setting and achievement of your ideas. You like your independence although you need to learn to involve yourself fully with people, and to allow yourself intimacy. You are a pioneer who breaks down perceptions and old ideas and you really 'go for life'.

You may be very withdrawn and insular, and never wander off your own path, or your own trail of thought. You may not like looking after yourself and become very dependent and refuse to believe you can achieve your goals. You may lose your direction in life at times.

1 LIFE PATH WITH A 2 PERSONALITY

With a 1 Life Path you are strong in your direction, ambition and leadership. This can influence your 2 Personality by helping you to make decisions (because twos can be very indecisive), and to lead in a caring manner. With a 1 influencing your Life Path you can be aloof and focused in your intellect. However, your strong mind can help you to be positive, when your emotions try to take you over. Your soft, caring and gentle (2) nature can help your mind to relax at the end of the day and when the going gets tough.

With a 1 Life Path, it can keep you stuck (1) by avoiding your emotions and relating (2) to people. You may remain stuck in your beliefs and outlook and prefer to work things out in your own way.

1 LIFE PATH WITH A 3 PERSONALITY

With a Life Path Number 1 you are strongly working on your independence and you have leadership skills. This can help your Personality Number 3, which has a tendency to be very scattered at times, to find a clear direction and focus.

Your Personality (3) is very light, fun loving, uplifting and joyous and can really bring some lightness to your day when things get too intense as they can when these two numbers mingle. Threes positively have a sunny and happy outlook on life, and this warmth can be channelled through your leadership (1).

You may have a tendency to overwork (3) and may become over preoccupied with your ability to lead and direct others (1). When both these numbers are being expressed with their negative influences, then there may be a great deal of distraction and

44   a lack of focus or concentration, and you may experience strong
emotions.

1 LIFE PATH WITH A 4 PERSONALITY

With a Personality Number 4 you are very methodical and like
to approach life in a step-by-step manner, as you are practical
and down to earth. When this couples with your 1 Life Path
Number it can really help you to materialize the goals which
you set for yourself. It can help you to carry them out slowly
and carefully and with determination and direction. Your 1 Life
Path can help to bring new direction when you get bogged
down (4) by life's problems and when you resist change (4).

The influence from the 1 in your Life Path can really bring out
the creative side in your Personality which sometimes gets lost
when you are over preoccupied with your own survival (4).

1 LIFE PATH WITH A 5 PERSONALITY

Your 5 Personality shows a quick-thinking and alert mind but
you can often change your opinion about things as you are very
changeable. Your 1 Life Path knows what you want and goes
about achieving it in a highly-focused manner. Therefore the 5
can influence your Personality by bringing you clarity about
what it is you want. Then you can go for these opportunities in
a directional (1) manner. You have a magnetic (5) Personality
which can make you a popular leader (1).

You are a champ at procrastinating and putting things off (5).
When this teams up with your lack of direction, at times, influenced by the 1 in your Life Path, you will really need to work
hard to keep your mind positive in order to get through challenging times of growth.

1 LIFE PATH WITH A 6 PERSONALITY  45

With the 6 Personality, you are very loving, caring, and nurturing, and you have a great appreciation of beauty. You like the good things in life – sensual clothes, fine art, music, food, etc. Your Life Path (1) can help to bring out this love of life by helping to drive you forward in your search for wholeness (6) by experiencing life to the full. You have a need to find your independence (1) within your community (6) – your family, local community, or the world at large – and make a good leader or representative.

Your 6 Personality likes to work with groups of people and your 1 Life Path likes to work alone, and in your own way. You may need to learn to accept others' leadership (1) or opinions when you are with a group (6) of people (at work, at home, etc).

1 LIFE PATH WITH A 7 PERSONALITY

With a 7 influencing your Personality, you (like your 1 Life Path) are a strong individual. You are able to get things going and make things happen easily when you are positive, and this can push you to drive forward with your direction in your Life Path (1).

With a 7, you can be drawn into your imagination, and with the influence from the 1 in your Life Path, you may become too lost in ideas and concepts. You can also be insular and like to be alone (1), and your Personality Number 7 can be introspective, and need space at times. If you are careful you can find a balance between doing, (with focus and direction), and being, (with enough time alone to think). Then you can create the space you need to help keep you happy.

1 LIFE PATH WITH AN 8 PERSONALITY

The strength with your 1 Life Path in your drive for independence can help to bring out the assertiveness and authority of

your 8 Personality. These two numbers together can bring great success particularly in business, where you may be extremely ambitious.

If at times you lack direction (1) and drive then your 8 Personality will bring back energy, and strength to help you refocus on your goals (1).

You can be a very powerful leader. However, with the influence of the 1 over your Life Path, it can also bring out a tyrannical side to your leadership. Then you may become bossy and self-driven by your greed (8) for power.

1 LIFE PATH WITH A 9 PERSONALITY

With a 1 influencing your Life Path, it can help to bring out the leadership with your teaching (9) skills, and you can teach others by the example you set. People often follow your example (9) and are inspired by your open mind and creativity.

Your 9 Personality will challenge your 1 Life Path to let go of your preoccupation with a goal or focus, and help you adapt to change, as both these numbers can bring in fresh ideas or direction.

These numbers together can mean that you may adopt your own (1) ways of doing things and 'make your own laws' (9), which can be impossible for others to follow.

HIGHLIGHTS OF NUMBER 1

POSITIVE	NEGATIVE
* Focused	* Unfocused
* Pioneer	* Destructive
* Independent	* Dependent
* Courageous	* Stuck emotionally
* Leader	* Self-centred

NUMBER 2

FAMOUS TWOS

HRH The Prince of Wales, Marvyn Gaye, Madonna, Phil Collins.

COUNTRIES

France, Germany, Africa, Tibet, United Kingdom, Venezuela.

GENERAL MEANINGS

Two is the number for balance and decision making.

PERSONALITY NUMBER 2

POSITIVE

With a 2 Personality you are highly sensitive and intuitive and have a gentle, quiet nature. You drink in life – you are open to others' suggestions and you make a good listener. Learning to listen is one of your key lessons and once you have mastered this you may attract many people to you for healing. You are able to relate to people – particularly through your emotions – where you feel safe to make contact with others.

With a 2 influencing your Personality you are able to nurture and care for others – like a mother – and you love to love others. You can be passive, soft and even pliable so that you become indifferent towards life, or at least not get het up about unimportant issues. You are good at making decisions, and will often put yourself into a position where you need to make choices (even difficult choices) in order to strengthen this quality.

You are placid, stable and able to steady others when they have problems. You are able to see both points of view or both sides of an argument. You also like both sides to 'win' when they are in situations of conflict, and like both sides to get their needs met. You believe that people can only sort out their problems by co-operating with each other and by 'working things out together'; arguing and fighting only causes more conflict and does not create a solution.

You are good at remaining calm and centred when others around you are crumbling, and will not take sides or be drawn into unnecessary arguments. You stay in the 'middle of the road'. With a 2 you are learning to be diplomatic in your speech, and to develop an unbiased view. You do not like to hurt people.

With a 2 influencing your Personality you are tolerant, and like sharing yourself with others. This can be sharing emotional exchange, sharing your possessions, sharing ideas, sharing your home, and so on. You believe simply that 'life is for sharing'.

You often like to compare yourself with others. This happens naturally because you like to see how you can relate to them, and how you can get along together.

You enjoy quiet pursuits, and you may have musical gifts which you use for yourself or to bring happiness to others.

NEGATIVE

With a 2 influencing your Personality, you can be a cautious person who takes life very slowly; you are not the type to dive into a new relationship or start a new career overnight! (Although at times you can 'throw caution to the wind'.)

You may be fearful of making decisions, perhaps because when you have made decisions in the past someone got hurt. (This may have been your parents when you were a child, who were both wanting you to do different things, and you had to choose between them.) With a 2 you can sometimes put pressure on yourself to make decisions, or put pressure on others to make decisions for you.

You can be defensive and confrontational, and constantly question people's opinions and decisions. You can also be highly disagreeable and awkward when you want to be, and you can be touchy at times.

With a 2 influencing your Personality you are a demanding person, particularly emotionally, and you need to feel needed by your partner, your friends, your family and your colleagues at work.

You can also be emotionally vulnerable at times, and want others to care for you and look after you. However, you are very good at looking after yourself and giving yourself warmth and nurturing, even though you may not want to sometimes.

With a 2 you can be uncaring towards others and when they need you (especially emotionally) you may walk away. You may not like or want to be an anchor for them and refuse to help them when they have problems to be sorted out. You can also be intolerant towards people when they are emotional, although you expect them to be able to tolerate you, and be patient with you.

You can be extremely moody, and you are very good at sulking. This causes a black cloud of heavyness for yourself and the people around you, because you are not able to express yourself directly. You draw people in at these times and bear down on people so that they feel pressurized.

With a 2 influencing your Personality you can be covert with your actions and you can even be deceitful. You may like to take sides when people are having arguments, just for the sake of it, and enjoy every moment. You may even take both people's sides (covertly) and agree with each one behind the other's back. You can also lack diplomacy and be tactless at times.

You can be highly uncooperative, and do not care about working things out with people, but prefer to get your own way. You may also be unable and unwilling to share your life with others, as you are still learning about 'give and take'.

With a 2 you are always comparing yourself with others, to see how you can make yourself feel good, or better than them.

LIFE PATH NUMBER 2

POSITIVE

With a 2 influencing your Life Path, you are learning to find balance within all areas of your life. You are working towards finding inner peace and calm, and learning to balance your emotions so that you have emotional stability.

NEGATIVE

There may be no sense of balance in your life. You may be emotionally weak, shaky or unbalanced, and your emotions may 'fly all over the place'. There may be general disharmony within your relationships as there is within yourself.

WISDOM NUMBER 2

POSITIVE

Your practical gift is the ability to share your love and wisdom with others; whether that be with those close to you, your community, or the world at large.

NEGATIVE

You may be unloving and uncaring and unable to share the knowledge from the experiences you have gained, in order to help others.

HOW THE NUMBER 2
INFLUENCES YOUR:

HEALTH

In terms of your health, with the influence of the 2, you are very aware about keeping a balance in your life, and try to do this at work, at play, by taking physical exercise, eating a healthy balanced diet, and getting plenty of sleep, etc. You are aware of your needs when it comes to balancing your mind, body and spirit. You may enjoy gentle meditation and yoga which helps to keep you calm, as much, if not more than physical exercise. Swimming is a key pastime and you love being by the water, which also helps to relax and soothe you. Keeping calm is essential as it helps keep your emotions balanced which is important for your whole health.

'Everything in moderation' may be your motto in your attempt to keep healthy, although on occasion you can be prone to over indulgence. Generally you are good at looking after and nurturing yourself, and you know how to be kind to yourself when you are under stress.

When you are sick you will generally take professional advice, although you only hear what you want to (especially if it's 'Go to bed for a week!') You may be very interested in complementary medicine and healing.

RELATIONSHIPS

With the 2 energy influencing your relationships, you are someone who is in love with being 'in love'. You are warm, loving and giving, and expect others to be the same. Finding a partner with whom you can share your life is important to you. You like being together and doing things together; perhaps to the extent of living and working together and spending most of your time together. This can be fun and a quick way to learn about sharing.

You are peace loving, and like your home environment to be peaceful and harmonious too. If your partner likes to play rock music at full volume every day forget it. You are sensitive to your partner's needs. Like a delicate, scented flower you need your partner to respect your vulnerability and your openness and sensitivity too.

You may be emotionally demanding with your partner, and over emotional at times. You may be oversensitive and take offence easily, even at the most innocent comment. You may feel rejected when you feel you haven't been heard, and perhaps you need to learn to listen to your partner. You may be someone who feels happiest when you know you are needed.

CAREER

The most important aspect within your career is to work in co-operation with your workmates; you like to feel you are working 'with' people, not 'for' them. You like working together with people on projects and sharing the load. As a career you would make a good judge or diplomat (because you are able to see both sides). You are an ideal 'middleman', agent, or a mediator within any organization or team. You would also feel at home as a counsellor (divorce counsellor, particularly), and in any community work or in the caring profession.

FINANCE

You are good at looking after your money, but you also know how to spend it when it is needed, especially if it makes your life more harmonious and smooth. You like to keep a balance between what you earn and what you spend, and you may even enjoy keeping your accounts or book keeping.

You can at times be overcautious with your money, and hoard it. At other times you can be extravagant and spend, spend, spend, particularly pandering to your emotional needs. When you feel upset you buy something to cheer you up. When you are happy you spend because you feel good, and when you are in a foul mood you may blow the whole lot in an hour! Having balanced emotions can help to keep your bank account balanced too.

HOW YOUR PERSONALITY AND LIFE PATH WORK TOGETHER

If your Life Path Number is a 2, look below and match it up to your Personality Number; these two numbers offer the strongest and most important influences over your life. Read a few key points about how your Personality and Life Path Numbers work together.

2 LIFE PATH WITH A 1 PERSONALITY

With a 2 Life Path you are working towards finding balance in your life. Your 1 Personality likes to strive ahead and will often focus for a long period of time (even many years) on one thing, to the extent of forgetting that there is any other life on planet earth. With the influence of the 2, it can help your ambitious Personality to stop and look around, and take a breather from times of intense focus (1). Alternatively, when you become unfocused (1), your Personality will say, 'Come on, let's find a goal and go for it.'

Your 2 Life Path means you are generally able to express your emotions; this can help encourage your 1 Personality to feel safe and feel intimate and go ahead and get deeply involved in relationships, and in life.

2 LIFE PATH WITH A 2 PERSONALITY

With a 2 Personality and a 2 Life Path, this intensifies the influence of this number in your life. You may be highly intuitive,

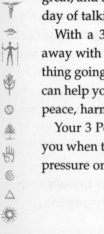

54   receptive and open, and really enjoy the simple life. You may like to wear a simple style of clothing, eat simple foods (you may even prefer raw foods), and be straightforward and simple in your approach. This is because you like and need harmony and peace in your life. You may even be happy living on a simple desert island with only a few people and animals for company, and with your own source of foods.

Wherever you choose to live, you know how to decorate your home to create a warm, inviting and peaceful environment, where people can feel relaxed and comfortable.

With a 2 Personality and Life Path you need to learn to balance your emotions; you may have mood swings varying from outbursts of emotion to sulking fits. However, you can also be placid and balanced and not let your emotions get the better of you.

2 LIFE PATH WITH A 3 PERSONALITY

With a 3 Personality you may be outgoing, expressive, joyous, and like a great deal of attention. You like chatting and comunicating with people and you are always 'on the go'. Your 2 Life Path can help to quieten you down and keep you calm. This is great, and at least you get to take a breather at the end of a long day of talking and 'doing'. What a relief!

With a 3 influencing your Personality, you can get carried away with being busy. You may be very scattered – with everything going in different directions at once. Here your 2 Life Path can help you by drawing in your energy, and this helps to bring peace, harmony and balance back into your life.

Your 3 Personality can support your 2 Life Path by uplifting you when things get too heavy (when you are putting too much pressure on yourself to do things).

With a 4 influencing your Personality you are particularly concerned with your material security and your physical survival. Your 2 Life Path is primarily interested in your emotional balance and well-being. Having physical security can help you to feel emotionally stable because you have roots which can anchor you when you feel upset. Being emotionally balanced can help you when you are moving home, for example, (4) because when you feel good (happy and balanced) you can handle life's challenges.

You can also find emotional harmony (2) from surviving (4) times of conflict, which can help you to become a more balanced person in the long run.

2 LIFE PATH WITH A 5 PERSONALITY

With the 5 influencing your Personality you are impulsive, quick-thinking and unpredictable. You can also be highly erratic and changeable at times. With a 2 influencing your Life Path it can help to bring peace to your mind (5) which can be overtaxed from thinking too much or from asking too many questions (you have an inquiring mind). When your mind leaps ahead to an idea or project your Personality may say, 'But how do I feel about that?', 'What is my gut instinct about this?' so that your mind and your emotions can make a joint decision.

Your 5 Personality can bring energy and vitality to your life when you get stuck on some emotional (2) issue that is unresolved. It can help by pushing you to express your emotions instead of bottling them up.

2 LIFE PATH WITH A 6 PERSONALITY

Your Life Path is influenced by the number 2, which means you care for peace and harmony, and your 6 Personality likes wholeness. In order to feel whole as a person you need to be able to

express your emotions and feel good in yourself before you can find balance in your life. This is how your 2 and 6 work together; by healing your emotions you can find new levels of wholeness within yourself.

With a 6 Personality you may be prone to obsession (with a project, a person, an idea, or a habit, etc). Your 2 Life Path can influence you positively by bringing in a sense of balance or proportion. This is so that you do not get carried away with the situation, or go around in circles, and get lost in your emotions.

2 LIFE PATH WITH A 7 PERSONALITY

With a 7 influencing your Personality you are someone who can be withdrawn into your imagination. With the influence from the 2 in your Life Path, it can help to draw you out of your mind and into physical reality, and help you to find balance (2).

Both your Personality and Life Path numbers influence your emotions, both are sensitive and can show vulnerability. However, both can also be strong and balanced if you learn to express your emotions and focus on the positive side of life. When your 7 Personality is thinking positively and your emotions are balanced then you are able to accomplish and materialize things very quickly, and harmony rings true in your whole life.

With the influences from the 2 and the 7, it can mean that you love swimming and spending time by the sea, by a lake, or waterfall or cruising up a river in a boat; water has a calming effect on your emotions and makes you feel good.

2 LIFE PATH WITH AN 8 PERSONALITY

With the influence of your 8 Personality you can be materialistic and love lots of possessions. You can be aggressive when you are trying to achieve this status of ownership. Your Life Path 2 can show you that by trying to possess things, it can actually create imbalances in the rest of your life. By having a balanced (2) approach to money (8) and possessions you can create emotional harmony and inner peace (2) in your life.

With the influence of the 2 in your Life Path, you can also be passive at times, and unbalanced emotionally. When your emotions go out of balance your 8 Personality can find it difficult to materialize your life – either a harmonious home, plenty of work, or smooth relationships.

2 LIFE PATH WITH A 9 PERSONALITY

With a 9 Personality you can be very idealistic in your outlook on life and how it 'should be'. When things are not as you think they ought to be you can get emotional, influenced by the 2 in your Life Path. The 2 can help you to view life in a balanced way, by helping you to accept life as it is, and by teaching you that even when things don't go the right way, there can still be emotional harmony in your life. When you feel centred and balanced things are more likely to 'go your way' anyway.

With a 9 you can also be rather self-indulgent, but your 2 Life Path can teach you that when you are emotionally balanced you do not need to indulge yourself in anything because you feel good the way you are!

HIGHLIGHTS OF NUMBER 2

POSITIVE	NEGATIVE
* Balanced	* Unbalanced
* Placid	* Cautious
* Decisive	* Indecisive
* Peace-loving	* Overemotional
* Kind	* Defensive

NUMBER 3

FAMOUS THREES

Katherine Hepburn, John Travolta, Linda McCartney, Barbara Walters.

COUNTRIES

Australia, Denmark, Luxembourg, Iceland, Vietnam, England, USA.

GENERAL MEANINGS

Number 3 is the number for expansion, moving forward, for protection, and abundance.

PERSONALITY NUMBER 3

POSITIVE

With a 3 Personality you are highly active both mentally and physically, and are usually bright and intelligent (although you may also choose not to develop your mind or use it to its full capacity). You are demonstrative, and fun is a part of your everyday routine. You have a witty, well-developed sense of humour that makes you very attractive. At parties people draw to you like magnets, where you are often the 'life and soul of the party'. You enjoy this, particularly because you crave attention, and like being on 'centre stage'. Indeed, you can keep people continuously entertained, and you are natural at acting!

People like you because you can make them laugh and make them feel good, and because you have a sunny, easy-going nature that uplifts them. You are confident and outgoing, with

an endless supply of free-flowing energy which you lavish on yourself and others. With a 3 you are an active person, and you consciously like to participate, and put as much into your life as possible.

You are usually bubbling with enthusiasm, and full of the joys of living. You know how to get along with different kinds of people, and you can talk to anyone – chat, chat, chat all day long sometimes! With a 3 you just love social contact. You also love romantic liaisons, food, and usually you love your work too.

With a 3 influencing your Personality you may like to wear bright, jazzy clothes which reflect your shining confidence. You are generally a 'laid back' person, so sports or casual wear may also appeal, particularly when you are relaxing. You may feel the most 'alive' in the 'great outdoors' and may enjoy camping, or activities such as riding, or trekking, etc.

You may have a strong connection and interest in mysticism – this does not necessarily mean witchcraft or folklore, but can cover any aspect of healing. You may also have strong religious beliefs which you may actively pursue, or you are simply aware of, in your life.

When challenges do arise in your life, you can usually cope really well because you simply take life in your stride.

NEGATIVE

With the 3 influencing your Personality you may experience a great deal of mental confusion at times. This can be because there are too many external factors influencing your life which all require your attention. For example, you may have put 'too many fingers in too many pies' and you just do not know what to do next. With a 3 you may also be confused because you have many conflicts going on inside you, which you do not understand.

60 Alternatively, with a 3, you can create confusion around you, and also create external conflicts in your life. You may even be in conflict with life itself, or even enjoy conflicts or create confusion in other people's lives too.

With a 3 you may be an untidy person who often 'gets in a mess', or leaves a mess behind you. For example, at home or in the office you can be untidy and messy, but you may also find yourself in 'messy' relationships, or think you 'make a mess' of them anyway. Sometimes you may even look a mess, or may be scruffy in the way you dress.

You may lead a chaotic lifestyle, rushing around and doing everything at once. However, you can sometimes dissipate your energy, and not accomplish as much as you'd like to in a day. You may lack the ability to focus on the important issues in your life, and end up doing things in a superficial way. With a 3 you also have a tendency to overwork, or overdo things at times.

Sometimes, with a 3, you can be so 'laid back,' relaxed and carefree that you don't get around to doing very much. You may be scattered, and lack boundaries or structure in your life; your lack of effort obviously bears little fruit.

With a 3 influencing your Personality you may suffer from a lack of confidence, which may stop you from doing things at times. You may find yourself constantly thinking, 'Can I, Can't I?' about opportunities that come your way. For example, a brilliant new position at work has been offered to you, which requires you to make regular speeches to many people. You think, 'Can I, Can't I?' as you have little confidence in your abilities. However, by saying, 'I can' you may actually gain confidence from each speech you make, which can positively affect your life.

You can be highly critical of yourself and others. This does not help your lack of confidence, but can make you feel worse, 'Oh you couldn't give that speech, aren't you stupid!' you may

say to yourself. You may also be highly critical of others too. Criticism is useless and can be destructive, because it knocks you down, and can lose you friends if you persist. However, constructive criticism is helpful, and can empower your life and drive you on to do better.

With a 3, you may lose your sense of humour, or your enthusiasm about your life. You can often join in critical or superficial gossip about others, and you will go out of your way to get attention for yourself, with the things you say.

LIFE PATH NUMBER 3

POSITIVE

With the 3 influencing your Life Path, you are learning about self-expression and creativity. Self-expression can be through your emotions, through physical activity, through your work, and through communicating. Your creativity greatly needs to be expressed, and another way you may do this is by using your hands. You are also a flexible person, who can adapt easily to changes in your life.

NEGATIVE

When you are strongly working through the negative elements of this number you may be unable to express yourself (at times) in one or many areas of your life. Your creativity may also be blocked. When your expression and creativity are blocked it can affect every area of your life. You may not adapt easily to changing circumstances around you.

WISDOM NUMBER 3

POSITIVE

With a 3 influencing your Wisdom Number, your practical gift is that of a positive mind. Keeping your mind positive means you help to create positive events in your life, and it helps keep other people positive too.

NEGATIVE

You may be burdened with negative thoughts, which may prevent your life from flowing in the best possible way.

HOW THE NUMBER 3 INFLUENCES YOUR:

HEALTH

Generally, with a 3 you are relaxed and laid back. A relaxed attitude helps you avoid taking on too much stress in your life, because you let go of worrying. This in turn helps you to stay healthy in the long run.

One of the ways stress may affect you is through your mind – when you become negative and confused about how to handle problems. At these times focusing on doing something you love may help to get you back on track. Turning towards the great outdoors, the active life, can also help you to relax; you may enjoy riding or cycling, etc. Another way you can relax is by having a good massage, which you find uplifting, as you also enjoy the physical touch.

With a 3 you can be scattered at times and not pay attention to what you are doing, so sometimes you can be accident-prone when your energy is going off in different directions.

Laughter is your best medicine, and your ability to feel joyous about life, no matter what, can help you find the positive side to any illness, and to life.

With a 3 influencing your relationships, your sense of fun makes you a great person to be with, particularly with your wicked sense of humour, and your flirtatious nature. You are magnetic and warm and enjoy the company of others.

You love to socialize with or without your partner, and whilst you can enjoy the company of one person (at a time!) you may enjoy many superficial and brief encounters too. You are a 'good time babe' and you may enjoy being carefree with your love.

With a 3, being able to express yourself in relationships is very important. In many ways it can be helpful for you to find a partner who is very 'down to earth' and grounded, if you are not like this yourself. This can help you with your whole life, and giving you boundaries can help to steady you when you become over-expressive.

When you feel it's time to commit yourself to a partner you will happily do so. Generally you are easy to be with, or live with, but be aware that not everybody enjoys criticism on a daily basis, even if they are your nearest and dearest.

CAREER

Any kind of career that enables you to express your creativity appeals to you; you may be an artist, a chef, a gardener, a massage therapist, physiotherapist, or a writer. You may be a professional socialite or a social worker. You may be involved with work that involves religion or mysticism, or you may well be a comedian, entertainer, tap dancer (you're light on your feet), or a (university) lecturer.

FINANCE

Number 3 has a strong association with abundance. When you have the potential for so much self-expression, and when all

your energy and enthusiasm are channelled into positive and hard work, money can simply roll in.

However, when you scatter your focus between too many projects, you also dissipate the energy which could be bringing you money. So money may wind its way into your bank account in dribs and drabs. Alternatively, if you have a little money coming in from many projects, this can make your account look very rosy indeed.

HOW YOUR PERSONALITY AND LIFE PATH WORK TOGETHER

If your Life Path Number is a 3, look below and match it up to your Personality Number; these two numbers offer the strongest and most important influences in your life. Read a few key points about how your Personality and Life Path Numbers work together.

3 LIFE PATH WITH A 1 PERSONALITY

With a 1 influencing your Personality, it can bring new ideas and freshness to the way you express yourself. For example, if you are an artist (3) and always paint in oils, your mind may say, 'Let's try watercolour and oils together this time,' and invent (1) some new way of working.

Your 1 Personality means you are dynamic with enormous amounts of energy focused upon a goal, and when this teams up with your 3 Life Path, your creativity can be expressed in a dynamic way too.

With a 1 Personality, you can also be determined to go along one route, or focus on one thing at a time. Then the influence of the 3 from your Life Path pops up, and asks you to be adaptable, and to focus on other things too.

With a 3 Life Path you are learning how to express yourself within every area of your life. When you are being passive (2) you will not want to come out and express yourself – particularly your emotions. The influence from the 3 in your Life Path can really help you to be more communicative, and help to 'free you up'.

The influence of the 3 in your Life Path means that you are adaptable. When you are faced with choices your 2 Personality can help you to weigh up the pros and cons, in order to make the best possible decisions about your life.

3 LIFE PATH WITH A 3 PERSONALITY

With a 3 Personality and a 3 Life path, it intensifies the qualities of the 3. This means, potentially, that you can make a great success out of expressing your creativity (maybe using your hands), as your gift. Perhaps you are a brilliant artist, or a prolific writer, or you have 'healing hands', or perhaps your gift is to be able to create an abundance of joy wherever you go.

With two 3s influencing your life you can be completely scattered, untidy, all over the place, and suffer from great outbursts of emotions. With two 3s in your chart you are 'happy go lucky' and really know how to enjoy yourself.

3 LIFE PATH WITH A 4 PERSONALITY

With a 4 influencing your Personality you are very grounded, practical and have the determination to go on and on. You work hard and keep at it until the job is finished. Your 3 Life Path also knows what it is like to work hard, but with great sparks of creativity. Together you can get a lot accomplished.

With a 3 Life Path, you can get creative in all different directions, and your 4 Personality provides a solid framework or structure in order to bring your creativity down to earth.

With a 3 Life Path and an earthy 4 influencing your Personality you may be someone who totally revels in expressing yourself physically. This can be by doing things with your hands, by being physically affectionate, by giving and receiving massage, by enjoying physical exercise, or by having fun with your partner.

3 LIFE PATH WITH A 5 PERSONALITY

With a 5 influencing your Personality, you are quick-thinking and you have a strong mind. You are a highly magnetic or attractive person. You can draw in an abundance of opportunities and situations where you can express your creativity (Life Path 3). This may be through work, through social expression or within your personal life.

With a 3 Life Path, you love self-expression and with a 5 Personality you love travelling and socializing. Together, you can have a really good time, and enjoy life to the full.

With the influence of the 5 in your Personality you can be changeable, which helps to teach your 3 Life Path to be adaptable to changes, and to take life as it comes.

3 LIFE PATH WITH A 6 PERSONALITY

With a 6 Personality you have a sense of wholeness, and you are continually learning to find wholeness within your life. You like to feel everybody is part of one group and that each of you plays an important part. The influence of the 3 over your Life Path means that you can work with your ability to express things, ideas, and issues on behalf of your family, your community, or at work. You can express the message which needs to be put across as part of the whole.

Threes naturally like fun, and you realize that being amusing in your self-expression can also help to make the whole (6) – or everybody – feel good too.

Your 3 Life Path with your 6 Personality means you can learn to express your love through a committed relationship, and can also express your love with friends and family too.

3 LIFE PATH WITH A 7 PERSONALITY

With a 7 Personality you have the ability to instantly materialize situations and things, which bodes well for your 3 Life Path. This is because it can help you to materialize the fruits of your creative expression. For example, you may decide you need to go on holiday, so your 3 Life Path paints a few pictures and sells them instantly (7). Your 7 Personality may also decide you would like your partner to take you to Paris for the weekend; you express (3) your desire to your partner and – Paris it is! Of course this doesn't mean you get everything you want in life, but you get what you need.

With a 7 Personality you can be prone to panic about things; your 3 Life Path is very laid back and learns to be adaptable when you panic, and encourages you to accept life as it is.

3 LIFE PATH WITH AN 8 PERSONALITY

Being stubborn and rigid are qualities you may experience with an 8 influencing your Personality. You may have a 'stiff upper lip' and like things 'just so'. Your 3 Life Path can help you by encouraging you to be flexible so that you can take each day as it comes.

Eight is also the number for authority and power, which can all be channelled through your creative expression (3 Life Path). Your paintings or writing may contain powerful messages. You may be a powerful chef who empowers a whole team of cooks at your disposal and encourages them to express their creative gifts through the food they serve. You may express your power in commerce by creating lots of business for your company's growth.

3 LIFE PATH WITH A 9 PERSONALITY

The influence from both the 9 in your Personality and the 3 in your Life Path, means you can be critical of yourself and others. Being critical means you do not accept life as it is – there is always something wrong. Constructive criticism is helpful from others, because it can improve your life. For example, you may be told you need to arrive at work on time because someone else is relying on you for your help. This is realistic criticism that can help to improve your relationship with your work colleagues, your work, and can help you feel happier in yourself.

Both your 9 Personality and your 3 Life Path can influence you so that you may have a keen interest in religion and politics. The 3 energy in your chart can help you to express your beliefs, either professionally through teaching (9) or lecturing, by expressing your beliefs to friends, or perhaps by writing about them or participating in events.

HIGHLIGHTS OF NUMBER 3

POSITIVE	NEGATIVE
* Adaptable	* Confused
* Self-expressive	* Lack of expression
* Creative	* Superficial
* Humorous	* Chaotic
* Communicative	* Uncommunicative

FAMOUS FOURS

The Dalai Lama, Richard Gere, Oprah Winfrey, Martina Navratilova.

COUNTRIES

Italy, Myanmar, Columbia.

GENERAL MEANINGS

Four is the number for foundations, grounding, systems – law and order.

PERSONALITY NUMBER 4

POSITIVE

With a 4 influencing your Personality you are someone who likes routine. You like to know exactly where you will wake up each morning, what your routine will be for each day, and when you make plans to do things, you generally do so well in advance. When travel schedules, meetings, and appointments are unexpectedly changed, it can really challenge you. Then you will try to fit them around your life, and return to your regular routine as soon as possible. You are happiest with a routine as you are a creature of habit.

The 4 influence means that each day you are learning about survival – how to 'chop wood, carry water'. But for you, knowing you can 'chop wood and carry water' every day is a blessing because it means routine. For you knowing your routine is

going to be the same offers you great security, and can help you to feel safe.

You are a home lover and a home maker, and putting down your roots and having a solid foundation from which to operate your life is very important to you. You like stability and you tend to think in terms of your long-term survival, or your long-term needs and future security. You are a provider, and can physically provide for yourself and others. You enjoy material comforts, and like to materialize things bringing your ideas into form.

You are happy to work hard to provide the lifestyle you require. You are persistent to the end, working in a step-by-step, practical manner with great determination to accomplish your goals. You are a highly capable person, and people know they can rely on you to follow through, once you have made a commitment or promise. You make a loyal friend, and although it may take you time to make friends, once you have established a rapport or a bond, then it's for life.

You are an eager beaver chopping away at life, and with each tree that falls, it helps to make your home a little sturdier, and safer. You also know you have many other trees to fell before you feel totally safe. Like a beaver you enjoy being in the woods, mountains, and you like to feel connected to the land.

You are tactile and earthy. You can be passionate and creative, and you are generally committed to your life and making it work.

NEGATIVE

With a 4 influencing your Personality you may dislike monotony. It is one thing having a routine but it's another when life seems to drag on the same today as it did yesterday, and with the same routine as tomorrow. Life is ordinary, and it is extraordinary, and it is up to you to make practical changes to help improve your life.

Change can be difficult for you to handle, because whilst you may welcome a change, or a break from your routine, it can make you feel insecure and uncomfortable. For example, moving home is one of the biggest changes you can face in your lifetime. It can make you feel very 'down in the dumps', because it challenges your physical security. When you resist change, you resist life, and you miss out on all the wonderful experiences which can colour your life, and make it enjoyable.

With a 4 influencing your Personality you may also be a workaholic, who hardly stops to eat. Perhaps this gives you great stability because it leaves you with no time to feel insecure. You may be fearful about your survival at times. For example, you may be fearful of redundancy at work, fearful about losing your home, etc, and this may lead you into a depression. To compensate, you may develop an all-consuming preoccupation with material possessions. You may hang on to things – clothes, cars, houses, books – and you may collect or even hoard things. Material possessions help you feel safe (or so you think).

Alternatively, with a 4, you may not wish to put your 'roots down' or to consolidate your life, and you may go through life with no real base or material security. You may endure life, rather than live life.

With a 4, you like everything 'in its place', and sometimes you can become too rigid in your approach to life. For example, if your partner left your books in the kitchen instead of on the bookshelf once too often, it could send you into fear and anger. However, when you introduce your own changes into your daily routine, you expect them to continue, and for everyone else to adhere to them. What a life!

You may be lazy and unproductive at times. You may plod on very slowly towards your goals. However, you do usually get there eventually. You can be very impractical. For example, you

may think you can finish baking a cake by teatime, but you forgot to add in the time it takes to go to the shop to buy the ingredients. With a 4 you can also be inefficient and may lack the persistence to carry things through.

With a 4 influencing your Personality you may find it difficult to form solid friendships, or be unprepared to put any effort into the ones you have already. You may also be disloyal to your friends, or feel hurt when they are disloyal towards you. With a 4, you may see friendships as a burden.

LIFE PATH NUMBER 4

POSITIVE

With your 4 Life Path your main direction or lessons in life are to learn to take responsibility for yourself and to learn how to master endurance, so that you can carry on no matter what. You are also learning to find satisfaction in the ordinariness of everyday living.

NEGATIVE

With a 4 influencing your Life Path you may display negative qualities of dissatisfaction within your life in general. You may be irresponsible and give up easily when challenges come your way.

WISDOM NUMBER 4

POSITIVE

With the influence of a 4 in your Wisdom Number, your practical gift is your ability to be able to consolidate your life. That is, you can take what you have made of your life, and build upon those experiences to make the ground firmer, and your life more solid.

The negative aspect of your 4 Wisdom Number means you may not be able to 'put your life down on paper' or make it firm, secure or real. Perhaps you do not have a firm base to work from.

HOW THE NUMBER 4 INFLUENCES YOUR:

HEALTH

You handle health problems in a practical way as you are a 'down-to-earth' person. You simply get on with your life each day by doing the best you can to help yourself get better. If you are told you are overweight then you may introduce exercise religiously into your daily routine. Usually, when you are told you need medication, then you take it, and on time. You keep plodding away with whatever helps.

At other times you can get quite angry or dramatic about taking time off to visit your dentist or health practitioner, perhaps because it interrupts your routine.

With a 4, you like your feet to be in contact with the earth and you enjoy getting your hands dirty doing the gardening, and it helps to relax you. You may also enjoy relaxation by rambling over mountains, or by going on a walking holiday. You may even take a pottery class because you love the feel of the clay, and love being able to materialize wonderful objects with your hands, and using your creativity.

RELATIONSHIPS

With a 4 influencing your life, friendship is the most important aspect within any relationship, including the relationship you have with your partner. You mate for life, and once you have found someone with whom you are compatible, as a companion

and friend, you are willing to put in much effort towards maintaining that union. You persevere, and even when there are problems you work very hard at sorting them out. When you have a steady relationship – a regular partner – it helps you to feel safe and secure.

You are practical and usually remember to buy cards and presents when it is somebody's birthdays or for a special occasion. However, you are not necessarily romantic, but if your partner likes to be given chocolates and flowers, then you are happy to oblige.

You like getting physical with your partner and enjoy the passion of creativity together. You are a home-maker and you may need a partner who also shares your love of home life. You may even prefer to do all your romancing at home, where you feel more secure, than go out to expensive restaurants or bars. You may even alternate dates between your home and your partner's home, or even enjoy nesting together.

CAREER

With a 4 influencing your career, you seek work that can offer you long-term security. You may be a housekeeper, a herbalist, a farmer. You may be a builder, a security officer, or work for an insurance or property company. Alternatively, you may work for a financial institution, or be an accountant.

With a 4, you like to think the company you work for has a strong foundation, or you may even build a foundation for them. Your need for security means that long-term employment, particularly with one company, may seem highly attractive to you.

FINANCE

With a 4 influencing your finances, then you are prepared to work hard for your money. You like buying material possessions

but you also like saving your money. You build upon what you
have in your bank account, which helps you to feel secure. You
can make yourself very financially comfortable indeed by
building upon your resources. This may be your aim rather
than looking to be incredibly rich (although with a 4 you may
never feel you have enough money to make you feel secure).

You may also like to invest money in property or 'secure'
bonds, which helps you to feel safe.

HOW YOUR PERSONALITY AND
LIFE PATH WORK TOGETHER

If your Life Path Number is a 4, look below and match it up
to your Personality Number; these two numbers offer the
strongest and most important influences over your life. Read
a few key points about how your Personality and Life Path
Numbers work together.

4 LIFE PATH WITH A 1 PERSONALITY

With a 4 Life Path you can bring endurance to your work to
help you finish it, because your 1 Personality can withdraw and
get lazy. For example, you may decide to work on a new project
that involves travelling. After two weeks of travelling you
just want to stay at home and withdraw, but your 4 Life Path
gives you the endurance to carry on until you have completed
the work.

Your 4 Life Path can help to make you more aware of taking
responsibility for your actions, and the focus you take within
your life. For instance, your 1 Personality may choose to lay all
your focus on your relationship with your partner, and with a
1 you do it fully. Whilst focusing on this you may forget your
work responsibilities as problems go unnoticed, work deadlines
fly by, and opportunities pass without you even noticing. With

a 4 Life Path you are learning to take responsibility for yourself within all areas of your life. With a 1 Personality you may also be self-centred and irresponsible (Life Path 4).

4 LIFE PATH WITH A 2 PERSONALITY

With a 4 Life Path influencing your 2 Personality you are able to obtain great satisfaction from sharing your life, and particularly your work, with others. You also feel satisfied when you are able to relate to people – to your friends, partner, family and workmates – because you feel connected. When people approach you with their problems, and you lend a kind 'ear', you find it very satisfying to be able to help them.

With the influence of a 2 in your Personality you can be cautious or careful, which can be a positive thing when you are about to make major decisions in your life. Your 4 Life Path can help you to take responsibility for the decisions you make so that you feel happy about them.

4 LIFE PATH WITH A 3 PERSONALITY

With a 3 Personality you are a bundle of laughs and you really know how to bring lightness and joy to your 4 Life Path, when you feel burdened and heavy with responsibility. For example, you may have been preparing information for an important company conference for weeks on end, and your 3 Personality will say, 'You deserve a break, come on, let's party!'

Similarly, your 3 Personality can be highly reckless at times, and irresponsible (4) at times, for example, by leaving your car headlights on, or forgetting to take your buns out of the oven. Your 4 Life Path gives you a little nudge and reminds you to take responsibility for your actions and to remember the consequences of such things!

With a 4 influencing your Personality and Life Path, this intensifies the qualities of the 4. You may be particularly aware of your responsibilities in life. You may be a highly creative workaholic, who has the endurance to carry on living 24 hours a day, and you methodically put a great deal into life.

You may be extremely materialistic with two 4s influencing your life. You are good at working hard and brilliant at earning money, and you can enjoy a comfortable lifestyle.

You are learning strongly about loyalty with these numbers, and you like to need to build solid friendships in your life, to help keep you feeling safe and stable.

4 LIFE PATH WITH A 5 PERSONALITY

With the influence of the 5 in your Personality you are someone who loves change and are changeable. Sometimes, however, it may seem like there is too much change going on in your life to comfortably handle. Your 4 Life Path can step in and help to give you the endurance you need to be able to carry on.

With a 5 Personality you may have a quick and a clear thinking mind. When you are about to be irresponsible (4) your mind steps in to help you. For instance, you may have tried jumping off a bus before it has completely come to a standstill. Your personality reacts quickly and says, 'Look before you leap!', so that you safely alight after the bus has stopped.

4 LIFE PATH WITH A 6 PERSONALITY

With a 6 Personality you are a loving and caring person. The influence from the 4 in your Life Path can help you to be responsible when you are nurturing others, and help you to take extra responsibility for looking after yourself. With the 6 and 4 together, you may have a desire for someone else to look after you. Everyone likes to be spoiled sometimes and it's lovely to

be brought breakfast in bed, as long as you know you are capable, and happy, to cook breakfast for yourself (and others) too.

Your 6 Personality may like to blame others when things go wrong. 'It's all their fault', you exclaim angrily, whilst negating any part you played in creating the situation. Your 4 Life Path can teach you to endure the results of your actions – everyone makes mistakes – and to take responsibility for the consequences.

4 LIFE PATH WITH A 7 PERSONALITY

With a 7 Personality you can be extremely evasive – that is, you avoid life and therefore try to avoid responsibility. For instance, you told your partner that you would go to a shop and pick up a watch that had been left for repair. However, that was on Monday and now it's Thursday, and whilst you have been a little busy at work you deserve an Oscar for avoiding any mention of the subject with your partner. This is avoiding (7) responsibility, and your 4 Life Path can teach you to face your responsibilities. This can help you to create more harmonious relationships with everyone in your life.

Alternatively, with a 7 Personality you are a deep thinker who thinks carefully about the responsibilities you take on.

4 LIFE PATH WITH AN 8 PERSONALITY

Both your 8 Personality and your 4 Life Path are good at taking responsibility. This can outwardly result in you materializing great success (8) within every area of your life. For instance, at work taking on more responsibility can be associated with promotion, which may increase your salary, and make you happier in yourself. When you are happier it positively influences every one around you; at home, at work, even in a traffic jam you are still smiling.

Education and learning are qualities contained within your 9 Personality. You like learning and you are able to teach and educate others too. With a 4 Life Path you can positively understand the responsibility that comes with teaching others and you will try to do it well. You also understand the responsibility of educating yourself or your children. You can educate yourself by learning something from everyone you meet, as well as learning in schools, colleges and at university. In fact life is full of lessons and everyone is in the same class.

With a 9 Personality and a 4 Life Path you may feel responsibility towards helping others in a selfless way. For example, you may take responsibility by doing the weekly recycling for your family and friends. Alternatively, you may be irresponsible in your attitude towards your environment, and be uncaring about how your actions affect others.

HIGHLIGHTS OF NUMBER 4

POSITIVE	NEGATIVE
* Responsible	* Irresponsible
* Down to earth	* Ungrounded
* Plodding	* Lazy
* Creative	* Insecure
* Comfortable	* Dissatisfied

NUMBER 5

FAMOUS FIVES

Mick Jagger, Paul Simon, John Cleese, Donald Trump.

COUNTRIES

Belgium, Wales, Spain, Sudan, Brazil, Saudi Arabia.

GENERAL MEANINGS

Number 5 is the number for experimentation, language, concrete knowledge or facts, and change.

PERSONALITY NUMBER 5

POSITIVE

With a 5 Personality you have a fascination with life – animal, vegetable, or mineral, it doesn't matter which. You have an inquisitive mind, and ask a lot of questions – you like to know facts and figures and what makes things tick. When children are growing up they are constantly learning, and fascinated because everything is 'new'. You are stimulated in a similar way; you thrive off change and new opportunities, and you 'go with the flow'. You like to make the most out of everything that comes your way because life is for exploring, and the more experiences you can have the better.

You love to learn about different subjects. You can have challenges choosing a subject to study, at university or at night school, because most things appeal. You can be like an encyclopaedia of general knowledge, having rounded up a little information about most things in life. You stop to taste things, and you are curious about life, but you may not always stay long enough to devour the whole thing. To you 'variety is the spice of life'.

You also have energy and a zest for life. Life is an adventure and you go out looking for it; you may love bungee jumping, white water rafting, scuba diving and skiing. These things excite you, make you feel alive and give you a thrill.

With a 5 you are a highly magnetic or attractive person, people are drawn to you because they sense your vitality. You are popular, and people are fascinated by you, and you are also fascinated by them! You ooze charm, and you enjoy flirting with everyone, even the cat! There are five senses and you like to explore every one of them.

You like to have fun, and one of your favourite pastimes is going to a party where you can rave and dance the whole night through. With a 5 you may also enjoy quiet dinner parties, where you can join in discussions about life, imparting some of the knowledge and information you have gained upon your 'journey'.

With a 5 you are a spontaneous person, and you can be as changeable as the wind. You love travelling; new people, new lands, new situations, new life … with so much to see and so much to do … non-stop.

NEGATIVE

With a 5 influencing your Personality you can be extremely restless. Your constant need to find new stimulation and new challenges sometimes drives you to distraction. You get bored easily and you need to keep your mind occupied to help keep you happy.

When your life does get 'in a rut' you may feel very frustrated, at work, at home, or on your everyday travels. You may find it difficult to settle down. At these times you can be prone to

making fast and sometimes irrational decisions, for example, walking out of your job or out of a relationship. You may feel like you want to create some excitement by running away, when in fact a simple holiday, or chat with a friend, may be all that you need.

With a 5, your impulsive nature can make you unreliable and unpredictable at times. For example, you may make appointments and turn up late, change the appointment, or not turn up at all. You can often change your outlook on life. You may also like to change your clothes often too, perhaps two or three times a day, or it can take you ages to decide what to wear at all.

You may be prone to stormy moods, or verbal outbursts, when you feel the frustration of not knowing where to go, or what to do next. There is so much choice, and life is constantly changing and constantly demanding you to be adaptable. You may also fear change. You may refuse to get on with your life, and procrastinate. Perhaps you say, 'I'll do it tomorrow', except tomorrow never comes, and life flies by.

With a 5 Personality you are also prone to setting yourself restrictions. For example, you may restrict yourself by saying 'I'll take x amount of money' during a job interview, when the company was going to offer a higher salary. You may restrict yourself by saying, 'I can only go out with somebody who has green eyes', so you miss out on all the other wonderful relationships you may have, because of this restriction. You may be scared to 'open up' to life, and use restrictions as a 'safety net' because it is overwhelming to realize there can be so much choice.

You can be like an ostrich and avoid facing facts and situations in your life. For example, you may not take too much notice about paying bills until the final demand lands on your doorstep. You may not even know what is in your bank account, or you may take overdrafts lightly.

You may sometimes be prone to addictions; chocolate, dandelion tea, food, alcohol, drugs, sex, people, etc, may all be methods of experimentation for you. You can also be abusive to people and towards things, and you can be very pushy at times.

With a 5 you may lack energy, vitality and enthusiasm, and lose your fascination for life, at times.

LIFE PATH NUMBER 5

POSITIVE

With your 5 influencing your Life Path, you are learning to express yourself through communication. Communication is important because it is the method by which you connect with others. You are also learning about commitment within all areas of your life. Another lesson from the influence of the 5 in your Life Path is to learn about freedom. This may mean you need your freedom, and you need to learn to allow others their freedom too.

NEGATIVE

With a 5 Life Path you may avoid commitment because you fear involvement or because you feel trapped (and you think you may lose your freedom). You may be unable to enjoy the freedom to communicate with others.

WISDOM NUMBER 5

POSITIVE

With a 5 influencing your Wisdom Number, your practical gift is your clarity of mind. You can use this gift to help others get clarity in their lives too.

NEGATIVE

With a 5 Wisdom Number you may experience mental confusion and, like a fog, be unable to see clearly the way ahead.

HOW THE NUMBER 5 INFLUENCES YOUR:

HEALTH

One of the best ways for you to keep your mind healthy is by keeping it focused and stimulated by learning new things. Reading books, studying, talking to people all help. A positive mind helps to attract positive situations, which can all help to keep you healthy.

With a 5 influencing your health, you are an active person and during times of illness you like to find out the facts, and get any 'niggle' about your health checked out. You may deluge your doctor with a list of questions. When you know the facts you can then take any necessary actions to help you get better; whether this be rest, medication or exercise.

For relaxation you may like to do a crossword, do stretching exercises at a gym, do a 'step' class, or go for a jog. Alternatively, you may also enjoy letting go by putting on some music at home, or by dancing away any stress. You love most forms of exercise but particularly skiing, skating, or roller blading, swimming, tennis and riding.

RELATIONSHIPS

With a 5 you are fun-loving, adventurous and lively and you may seek out a partner who shares your same zest for life. You may also like a partner who can offer you intellectual stimulation – someone you can share interesting conversations with over dinner.

You are attractive, flirtatious and make friends easily (but at times you may also disregard them easily too). You live your life in the fast lane, enjoying your freedom and sensual pleasures.

With a 5, when you make a commitment to your partner, it can help you to curb your restlessness, and can help you learn that it is possible to find your freedom within a committed relationship. For example, you may feel the urge to take a month off and go travelling abroad without your partner. You may enjoy a few social evenings every week alone with your friends, as well as socializing with your partner. Even when you are married you can still enjoy your own identity and do things on your own.

However, it is possible that you may not like to get involved too deeply with one person because you can feel trapped. You may prefer to flit about so that you have a variety of experiences and experiment with your life.

CAREER

With a 5 influencing your career you are likely to excel in anything related to the communications industry; public relations, marketing, sales, journalism, travel, computing, etc.

You can also make a brilliant investigator, manager, travel guide (or writer), dancer, or even a disc jockey. You may be a teacher or you may work with languages, perhaps as a translator.

FINANCE

Once you have learned to commit to life and to a career you may earn plenty of money – and fast. However, you may also spend it as fast as you earn it. Spending money can become another addiction, because you love life and there are so many things you need to do, and they all require money. However, you are magnetic and there is usually more where the last lot came from.

With a 5 you may find that money comes in chunks, so you may go from overdraft to having plenty in your bank account. You may enjoy taking a risk with your money, perhaps buying stocks and shares and gambling with your financial 'wheel of fortune'.

HOW YOUR PERSONALITY AND LIFE PATH WORK TOGETHER

If your Life Path Number is a 5, look below and match it up to your Personality Number; these two numbers offer the strongest and most important influences over your life. Read a few key points about how your Personality and Life Path Numbers work together.

5 LIFE PATH WITH A 1 PERSONALITY

With a 1 Personality you enjoy developing your intellect and with the influence of the 5 in your Life Path, you really enjoy intellectual communication with others. With the 1 and 5 together you may have a very sharp mind, with a dry wit.

With a 5 Life Path you often feel the need for freedom and when your 1 Personality has been focussing on something for too long then your 5 will say, 'Take a break.' This can be helpful, particularly if you haven't eaten all day! Alternatively, when your 5 Life Path is running off in all different directions your Personality can help to focus you and get you 'back on track'.

With your 1 Personality you like to pioneer new ground and your 5 Life Path can help you with the commitment to follow your ideas, and to go for your dreams. Pioneering may mean starting a new relationship, travelling over new ground (literally), inventing new jobs or new ways of doing things, etc.

With a 2 Personality you are someone who likes to relate to others, and your 5 Life Plan likes to communicate. So, together, you are a real 'people's person' who may be able to communicate in a gentle, caring and diplomatic way. With the influence of your 2 Personality you can make an excellent counsellor where you are able to listen (2) carefully to what others need to communicate (5).

With the influence of the 5 in your Life Path, you may be someone who does not like to get too involved with people emotionally, which may conflict with your 2 Personality who loves emotional contact. However, you can learn to gently allow yourself to feel safe with your emotions, and when your mind (5) is strong, it can help give you emotional stability (2) and make you happy.

5 LIFE PATH WITH A 3 PERSONALITY

With a 5 Life Path you are freedom loving, and you like to communicate – you make an excellent speaker. Your 3 Personality loves self-expression, so with the free-flowing vital energies of the 3 and 5 together you really know how to let the world know you are here! You can make an excellent translator, and excel in the communications field. You also like to chat a lot, so with the attraction of the 5 you are likely to have lots of friends who like chatting too!

Both the 5 Life Path and 3 Personality are freedom loving, and the lightness and joy of the 3 coupled with the adventure and spark of the 5 can mean you are great fun to be around. Whatever you are doing – cooking, writing, looking after children, working – you can totally immerse yourself in the fun and adventure of it. Life is for living, and you enjoy your 'happy go lucky' nature.

5 LIFE PATH WITH A 4 PERSONALITY

With a 4 Personality you like to have your feet firmly on the ground and you like to feel secure. However, with a 5 influencing your Life Path you may be someone who likes your freedom, and this can create conflicts in your life. That is, until you learn that you can take off into the horizon and have stability as well.

With a 5 Life Path you do not always relish taking on commitments. However, with the 4 influencing your Personality you can be good at making commitments that are rock hard and steady. For instance, your personality may have made a commitment to the company you work for and after 14 years you are still there; this offers you security. But your 5 Life Path may mean that you make a commitment, and after 5 minutes want to change it! The 5 can help you to work on this by taking and committing to each day as it comes. Your Personality then brings in the determination to help you get through.

5 LIFE PATH WITH A 5 PERSONALITY

With a 5 influencing your Personality and your Life Path this intensifies the qualities of the 5. You may have an enormous gift for communicating and use this in your career. You may make a life out of travelling the world and having adventures. Perhaps, on the other hand, you are brilliant at taking on commitments and you stay put right where you are. Each commitment can be an adventure and you can thrive off each one.

With two 5s influencing your life you are an ace at procrastinating and if ever the freedom bug bites you, watch out because you may be so restless that you don't ever sit down! With two 5s in your chart life can't possibly get boring for very long.

Six is a number very strongly associated with relationships; relationships of every kind including with animals. With a 5 influencing your Life Path you are learning about commitment (6) within your relationships – with a partner, with your family, and with your work colleagues and friends. When you are in a committed intimate relationship you can still feel 'free' and you can allow your partner freedom too. This is important and by having your freedom you do not feel restricted (5).

With a 5, you can find wholeness (6) within a relationship where there is freedom and commitment. You are very communicative (5). By communicating to your partner when you may feel trapped, it can help you to resolve the situation, and enter into deeper levels of commitment.

5 LIFE PATH WITH A 7 PERSONALITY

With a 7 influencing your Personality you are someone who may panic when you have to make any kind of commitment (5), and you may feel trapped. You are very sensitive, and can feel emotionally vulnerable at times. The 5 can influence your Life Path by encouraging you to talk through your fears of commitment with your partner, friends or family, to find the reality in your fears. When your 7 Personality and 5 Life Path combine to create positive thinking, you can produce an enormous amount of opportunities for you to commit to.

Your 7 Personality can positively enjoy the freedom to explore (5) your mind and imagination, rather than the freedom to roam around the world literally (although you may do this as well). As a result of your vivid imagination (7), you can be wonderfully creative in your communications with the world. You would, for example, make a popular narrator, or children's storyteller.

5 LIFE PATH WITH AN 8 PERSONALITY

Your Personality 8 like your Life Path 5 both carry qualities of animal magnetism. This may bring success to practically anything you try to do especially in your career as you have a flair for business. However, you are prone to being manipulative (8) in your communication (5) when trying to achieve your goals, and you can be aggressive and arrogant (8) when you do succeed.

With an 8 Personality you aim to be responsible with what messages you communicate (5), at work particularly, where you may be responsible for influencing many people. With the influence of the 8 in your Personality you can be very successful but you may take on too many commitments (5). Then your 5 Life Path may say, 'let's lighten the load' and encourage you to delegate your responsibilities to others.

5 LIFE PATH WITH A 9 PERSONALITY

With a 9 influencing your Personality you are someone who may have strong opinions and beliefs about life, and how it 'should' be, because you are idealistic. Your Life Path 5 can help you to express your beliefs and communicate them to others. For example, you may think that a new photocopier at work would really help you. There would be fewer arguments over 'who's using it next', and because it would work properly then it would save time and efficiency. You communicate your belief to your boss. A new photocopier is purchased, which helps to improve your life, and everyone else's, including your boss's.

With a 9 Personality you can also be highly critical and may influence people with negative communication (Life Path 5), by moaning and complaining about life (including the photocopier!)

HIGHLIGHTS OF NUMBER 5

POSITIVE	NEGATIVE
* Communicative	* Uncommunicative
* Freedom-loving	* Restriction
* Adventurous	* Impulsive
* Magnetic	* Addictive
* Curious	* Procrastinate

NUMBER 6

FAMOUS SIXES

Joan of Arc, George Michael, Howard Hughes, John Lennon.

COUNTRIES

Mexico, Thailand, Russia, New Zealand, Japan, Norway, Canada, Iran.

GENERAL MEANINGS

Number 6 is the number for harmony, commitment, relationships, marriage and family.

PERSONALITY NUMBER 6

POSITIVE

With a 6 Personality your home is one of the most important aspects within your life, and is always at the centre of your attention. You love being at home and indeed you may revel in domestic bliss. You may even work from home, so that your career and personal life can be fulfilled in an environment that brings you great joy and emotional security. Work, meetings, parties, music, colour, the perfume of flowers fill the air – your home is often a hive of activity where people can work out their relationships. Your home is a place of wholeness where everyone can fit in to the whole picture and play their part. Wholeness is an important issue, and you are learning to find wholeness within yourself and through your relationships.

Family life is essential to your enjoyment of life; you enjoy being part of a group. You take your family duties seriously and

enjoy helping – you are always helping others. You are a carer, who loves to look after and nurture people, and you make a good listener. People are drawn to you and often tell you their problems and 'life story', which you love because it helps you to develop a larger perspective on life.

You are a loving, warm, generous person and you are good at giving. You are highly perceptive and can see other people's needs; the needs of your family, of your community and the world at large. You may work for a charity, and when you see a problem, you are greatly moved to help and are devoted to that cause. Indeed you are a crusader with a keen sense of justice.

With a 6 influencing your Personality you have a strong desire for the good things in life – good food and wine, fine and colourful art, harmonious music, beautiful fabrics and clothes, etc. You are usually highly fashion conscious, and enjoy trips to art galleries, concerts and to the theatre. You have an appreciation of beauty and aesthetics and you are sensitive to your environment. You like to 'feel' life, to feel people, and you like to feel good; emotional harmony is essential to your happiness.

With a 6, you can be an idealist and perfectionist at times, but you also like to meander through life and just 'let yourself go'. You like to go deeply into life; in your relationships, at work, etc. You can commit yourself fully.

NEGATIVE

With a 6 influencing your Personality you may resent your duties, and resent looking after and caring for people. This applies to looking after your partner, your family, friends, or someone within your community. You can feel resentful sometimes, because you feel like you have no choice, and that you 'have to' carry out your duties. For example, your aunt asked you to pick up a magazine from the shop for her, but it means travelling across town. You may do it but feel so angry and

94   resentful that it ruins your whole day. When you do things with a 'cold heart' it doesn't help you or others. You may even neglect your duties at times, or try to opt out of your commitments.

You can be overgenerous, and help everyone who comes your way, 'Yes I'll finish that project for you, yes I'll pick you up from the airport, yes I'll do your shopping', etc. Perhaps you need to learn to say 'no' sometimes and prevent yourself from becoming a willing doormat and being taken for granted. You have a kind heart but helping people can leave you breathless, with no time to yourself, or time to get on with your own life.

With a 6 you may also be a moaning martyr who continues to help people, whilst letting the whole world know what a saint you are! You may moan, 'Poor me, look what I'm doing for everyone.' Alternatively, you may be a silent martyr who goes around with a troubled face, thinking to yourself, 'Poor me, poor me.'

You can be interfering at times, and you may want to get overinvolved with people's lives, particularly emotionally. You may emotionally smother others, by constantly wanting to know what they are feeling. With a 6 you may be overemotional at times, and very 'needy'. You may easily get emotionally attached to people; and let your feelings run away with you. When someone hurts you emotionally you may like to 'get your own back' and even be vengeful at times.

With the 6 influencing your Personality you can go very deeply into life and may even develop obsessions about things – your work, your health, the way you look, the food you eat – or you may become obsessive about a person.

Obsessions create disharmony within your life, but when you release an obsession it can help you to feel whole again. For example, you may have an obsession with your weight; perhaps you are underweight and you are constantly worrying about it. After a short time you may get so fed up with piling down food to try to put on weight that one day you simply give up. You stop obsessively worrying about your weight and decide to accept your body the way it is. Releasing an obsession can help to bring your mind, body and spirit back into harmony, and into wholeness.

With a 6 influencing your Personality you are also prone to jealousy. Sometimes when you are jealous it is because you are not acknowledging your own gifts or seeing goodness within yourself.

LIFE PATH NUMBER 6

POSITIVE

The main influences from the 6 in your Life Path are your ability to take responsibility for the group (your family, community, etc) and to recognize group needs. Also to use your wisdom to help yourself and others, and to use your gift of healing. You are learning about all these qualities to help you with your life.

NEGATIVE

With a 6 Life Path you may recognize others' needs but only be interested in getting your own needs met. You may find it difficult to take on family responsibilities or refuse to take on group responsibilities. You may feel uncomfortable sharing or using your wisdom to help heal yourself and others.

WISDOM NUMBER 6

POSITIVE

With a 6 Wisdom Number, you have a practical gift of tolerance which helps you to learn to 'live' with people and accept life as it is.

NEGATIVE

You may experience challenges by being intolerant, and not accepting other people's feelings, or accepting people and things as they are.

HOW THE NUMBER 6 INFLUENCES YOUR:

HEALTH

With a 6 influencing your health you are generally very aware of your diet – food is an important focus for you. For you food is strongly associated with emotional security and helps you to feel good. You may enjoy cooking, and love to have family or friends around a big table to enjoy the 'spoils of nature'. It is possible that wholefoods or organic foods feature strongly in your diet. You like the 'good life' and you may be inclined to overindulge yourself in food.

When you are ill you may feel very sorry for yourself, whilst at the same time take good care of yourself, or you may want others to wait on you 'hand and foot'. Sometimes, even when you are ill, you are still aware of others' needs and may go out of your way to help them if you can.

For relaxation you enjoy having a sumptuous facial, manicure or massage – you love to be pampered. Picnics in the park and outdoor concerts also help to relax you and keep you happy. You keep fit by participating in team exercise, like rowing, tennis, basketball, and so on, where you feel part of a group. Whatever you do you like to do it well.

RELATIONSHIP

With a 6 influencing your life, you like to get emotionally involved with your partner and to go deeply into the relationship, by making a commitment. You can bring love and affection into any relationship, although you may also neglect caring for your partner at times.

You are one of nature's true romantics. You were born to be showered (or to shower others) with flowers, expensive perfumes and gifts, and to you this is an expected part of any relationship. You enjoy walking along the moonlit beach and being serenaded with violins over dinner. You are a professional. However, you can be idealistic in the way you view your partner. In the 'honeymoon' period you may feel emotionally secure and happy, but you may shy away from commitment when you eventually notice things are not as ideal as they once appeared.

Family is an important issue to you. This can mean that you have a strong desire for your own family, or that the family to which you were born plays a big role in your life. With a partner you may have a strong urge to settle down, because 'home is where the heart is'.

CAREER

You have a strong sense of duty and responsibility for your community, and you can make a good charity worker, or community carer. You may succeed in the litigation field (because you are able to see the whole picture), and can excel as a marriage guidance or children's counsellor. You may also work in the medical profession where you enjoy taking on responsibility for others.

With your love of aesthetics you may also be a (graphic) artist, beautician, musician or singer, colour therapist, writer, or a designer of any sort. You may also become a vet, because you have a love and compassion for animals too.

FINANCE

With your love for wholeness, you earn money not simply for the sake of it, but as a method to provide you with the good

things in life. For example, you like to buy nice clothes, good food, perfumes, flowers, take lovely holidays, and to live in lovely surroundings.

With a 6 you are very good at providing money to care for yourself, but a part of you may also like someone else to provide money for you. You do not always enjoy working for a living.

Whether you work hard for your money or not, finding wholeness within your life can still mean there is plenty in your bank account, even if you did inherit it!

HOW YOUR PERSONALITY AND LIFE PATH WORK TOGETHER

If your Life Path Number is a 6, look below and match it up to your Personality Number; these two numbers offer the strongest and most important influences over your life. Read a few key points about how your Personality and Life Path Numbers work together.

6 LIFE PATH WITH A 1 PERSONALITY

With a 1 Personality you are self-centred and think only about your own needs. With a 6 Life Path you generally think in terms of group responsibilities; what is best for your family, group and for everybody concerned. Together the 1 and 6 can influence you by helping to balance each other out, so that you can enjoy taking responsibility for yourself and others.

With a 6 Life Path you are a wise person and that wisdom can shine through when you are focusing (1) on important issues or projects. It can help you see the best way to move forward when you are pioneering new ideas (1) or projects. You have gained wisdom by life's experiences and you can gain more wisdom by experiencing new things (1).

With a 2 Personality you are learning to make decisions, and when that is influenced by the 6 in your Life Path, you may be very good at taking responsibility for making group decisions. For example, you may work as a trader selling commodities on a trading floor in a bank. When you sell or buy something you take responsibility for making the best decision for the whole group; your client, your company and the third party on the telephone.

With a 2 influencing your Personality you may be moody and sulk at times, and you can be emotional. You may find great healing (6) by listening to music or playing the piano, to help you contact and express your emotions.

6 LIFE PATH WITH A 3 PERSONALITY

With a 6 Life Path and a 3 Personality you can help to heal yourself and others with your sense of humour and your ability to uplift and inspire others with your *joie de vivre*. Wisdom (6) may be expressed through your jokes (3) and can help to teach others about life, so that they feel wiser too.

With a 3 Personality you can sometimes feel confusion or inner conflict, and you are unable (6) to take responsibility for your family, work colleagues or group. This can last for 5 minutes, a week or for many years.

However, by taking on group responsibilities there is no time to be confused because you have too much to think about. When the confusion lifts, your sunny nature shines through and your spirit lightens everyone around you.

6 LIFE PATH WITH A 4 PERSONALITY

With a 4 Personality you are generally solid, dependable and secure. With this solid base you can easily and happily take on enormous amounts of responsibility (6) for your community,

within an organization, or for your family. On the other hand, if you are feeling insecure, you may resist taking on additional (6) responsibilities because with them comes change, and you prefer to stick with your daily routine (4).

With a 4 Personality you may sometimes feel insecure or fret about your survival, 'Do I have enough money? Do I have enough food to eat? Will I still have a job tomorrow?' With a 6 Life Path you are full of inner wisdom. When you are worried, it can help to guide you to take the appropriate actions to face your situation, and to help you feel safe.

6 LIFE PATH WITH A 5 PERSONALITY

With a 5 influencing your Personality you have a strong fascination for life, and an inquiring mind that likes to know how things work, and what makes people 'tick'. With a 6 Life Path you are full of wisdom. Your Personality can drink in that wisdom and add to your worldly experiences (5) the inner knowledge which the 6 brings.

With a 6 Life Path, you can help to bring healing to your Personality when you are restless (5) and unable to settle down. It can help you by calming your mind and encouraging you to feel positive about your life. Then life can simply unfold without you feeling the need to run away (5) from your responsibilities (6), by being restless and non-committal.

6 LIFE PATH WITH A 6 PERSONALITY

With a 6 Personality and a 6 Life Path the influences from this number are intensified, so that you can learn about them fully. You may be very warm, affectionate and loving, with a generous nature, and use this in your work where you care for others. You may be a brilliant artist or writer, and bring much healing to people with your creative talents.

With two 6s influencing your life you are a group player who may try to find wholeness by working or living with different types of people, and by exploring relationships. Home life and family are doubly highlighted here, which may challenge your responsibilities and be an important issue to you.

6 LIFE PATH WITH A 7 PERSONALITY

With a 6 Personality you are ace at bringing people together and making things happen. You may take on a group responsibility (6) by organizing a 21st birthday party for your brother which brings all your family, friends, and long-lost relatives together. Much healing (6) takes place, and you can certainly be pleased that you accepted that particular group responsibility, which was great fun.

With a 6 you can also be irresponsible, and with a 7 Personality you can be dreamy and avoid facing up to the reality of your family or group responsibilities.

6 LIFE PATH WITH AN 8 PERSONALITY

With the 8 influencing your 6 Life Path you are someone who can be inspired by taking responsibilities for others. This is because responsibility drives you on to do better, and to succeed in every area of your life. You are materialistic (8) and taking on more responsibility (6) can also mean that you have more money for yourself and for others. For example, you may be a fashion designer who takes on a group responsibility by bringing in a new business partner. It benefits the whole company because this brings in extra work, and more money for you and your workmates.

With an 8 Personality you can possess a great flair for business, and with a 6 influencing your Life Path, you can apply your wisdom to your work. This can help to guide you on to further success (8).

PRINCIPLES OF NUMEROLOGY

6 LIFE PATH WITH A 9 PERSONALITY

With a 9 Personality and a 6 Life Path you may be a teacher or leader who can teach yourself and others how to take responsibility for family or for the community you live in. For example, you may teach people about the environment and illustrate to them the need to share the responsibility for making the world a better place to live.

You may receive healing from listening to your own wisdom (6) and then use this knowledge to help heal others. For instance, if you are a marriage guidance counsellor, you may gain inner wisdom from the hundreds of people you have helped over the years. This knowledge can help to heal you and can also help to heal others.

HIGHLIGHTS OF NUMBER 6

POSITIVE	NEGATIVE
* Loving	* Uncaring
* Just	* Unjust
* Responsibility for group	* No group responsibility
* Generous	* Mean
* Idealistic	* Obsessive

FAMOUS SEVENS

Lauren Bacall, Roger Moore, Marilyn Monroe, Bruce Lee.

COUNTRIES

Sweden, Greece, Bolivia, Peru, Scotland, Philippines, Netherlands.

GENERAL MEANINGS

Number 7 is the number for rest, reality, fusion, magic and materialization.

PERSONALITY NUMBER 7

POSITIVE

With a 7 Personality you are someone who is highly intuitive, and you may even be telepathic. Having strong intuition and instincts can help you when you need to make important decisions about your life, and with your day-to-day living. You have realized that by following your inner guidance your life really seems to flow. You are a sensitive person and when you walk into a room you can pick up on the mood instantly. You have a protective streak within your Personality, which you may use for yourself (when you are feeling vulnerable), or towards others.

You are methodical and very organized, and you are also courteous. Good manners are important to you and you always like to remember to send thank you cards. You are analytical and a perfectionist, and you may pay great attention to detail.

This can reflect in the way you dress because you are often fastidious in your appearance. With a 7 you are naturally a tidy person, and at the end of the day you like to have a clear desk and a tidy kitchen.

You are an introspective person who likes time to think and ponder on life, and you may like to keep a diary or journal where you can write down your thoughts. You are a private person. With a 7 you can be a loner who needs your own space or 'cave', where you can withdraw into your mind when life gets too hectic.

You can be dreamy, and you have a vivid imagination which makes you particularly affable and good with children. You are nature loving and you love all the colours in the rainbow. You love each season and you realize that life has its own natural rhythms in which you play a part.

With the 7 influencing your Personality you are an instigator, with the practical ability to materialize things and make things happen 'at the drop of a hat'. You project an air of wealth and even when you don't have pots of money in the bank people think you do! However, you do have a penchant for the 'best' and you are likely to pick the most expensive item on the menu when dining out, without even noticing the cost!

With a 7 you can also be very spiritual and have a keen interest in the 'New Age', its concepts and ideas.

NEGATIVE

With a 7 influencing your Personality, you are someone who is self-centred, and who views others by how their lives are going to affect you. You can be too introspective at times, and can also be self-absorbed to the extent that you fail to notice any other life on planet earth! Learning to be aware of people around you, and of other people's needs, can help you to keep your two feet on the ground, and keep you in reality.

You may be a loner who often feels isolated, distant, disconnected from people, and cut off from life. You can be emotionally cold at times, and feel unable to reveal your feelings, even to the people you know. At other times you may overexpress your emotions, so that they flood out of you at a fast pace. When your emotions do get the better of you, you can be prone to 'doom and gloom', particularly with your strong mind, which can wander into a downward spiral of negativity about your life. At these times you are likely to pour out your feelings and negative thoughts to everyone you meet, so that they also get a dose of 'the blues'.

With 7 you are a dreamer, lost in a life of illusion, where you may prefer to live out your life in your imagination rather than in the real world. At these times you may float around, with no real substance to you at all; the lights are on but there's nobody at home.

You may have a tendency to 'sit on the fence' when opportunities come your way, and watch them drift by, as life slips through your fingers. Indeed, you may be a voyeur who prefers to take a 'bird's eye' view on life, rather than get involved. With a 7 you can be evasive, and evade life by refusing to ground yourself and live in the physical world.

Alternatively, at times when you are 'down to earth', and living in the real world, you can develop an overriding preoccupation with making money and material possessions.

A 7 can make you a difficult person, who is picky and notices every little imperfection; you have impossibly high standards at times. With a 7 you may also have an inferiority complex and never feel 'good enough', at anything.

You often feel hypersensitive and emotionally vulnerable. At these times you may try to overprotect yourself from life, situations and people, even when there is no real need. When you are feeling vulnerable you may also feel you want others to protect you too.

At times when you are feeling sensitive you can sometimes be rude to people, hurtful, and even lash out by being cruel. Often you do not realize you are being insensitive or hurting others, because you are so immersed in yourself. With a 7, you can also be oversensitive and take others comments too personally, and you are easily hurt. You can be naive, and have a childlike view of the world, and can often be 'taken in' by life and people.

LIFE PATH NUMBER 7

POSITIVE

With a 7 influencing your Life Path you are learning to appreciate what you have, and to appreciate life. You are also learning to trust yourself and to trust others, and to find your own truth in life.

NEGATIVE

With a 7 Life Path you are impatient and distrusting of people and life. You may evade the truth or be untruthful, and you may take life for granted and show a lack of appreciation towards others.

WISDOM NUMBER 7

POSITIVE

With a 7 Wisdom Number your practical gift is being able to visualize things very clearly. You are a visionary who has strong intuition and you often receive your guidance through visual dreams.

With a 7 influencing your Wisdom Number you are unable to see clearly, or 'see through' situations or people, and do not follow your intuition or inner vision.

HOW THE NUMBER 7 INFLUENCES YOUR:

HEALTH

With a 7 Personality you are generally robust, but as a result of your sensitive nature your health can also be sensitive and can be fragile and delicate at times, too. That is, when you are feeling 'low' your body can slip out of balance quickly and you may get sick. At the same time your sensitivity is helpful because you may react very quickly to medicines and healing, and your body can often balance itself out. With a 7 you pay fine attention to your health, but you can become too preoccupied with every little sneeze, ache and pain.

To help keep you fit, you may exercise by playing tennis, and swimming (with dolphins), particularly in the summer sun, where you apply copious amounts of sun tan lotion to protect your sensitive skin.

You love being by the sea, lakes and waterfalls, and may enjoy lazy days spent drifting on a boat up the river. You love trees, and flowers – indeed you appreciate all of nature.

For relaxation you may absorb yourself in a book, do needlework, or immerse yourself in meditation. You may enjoy Tai Chi or gentle Yoga, which can help you to keep your delicate energies balanced.

RELATIONSHIPS

In relationships you are very choosy, and will wait for the right person to come along before you settle down. You have a strong

mind, and when you set your sights on finding the best possible partner for yourself, half a dozen may instantly appear!

With a 7 space is a very important issue, because without space it is a challenge for you to stay centred. For example, when you constantly have people around you it can actually make you feel ill. This is because you need space to internalize what happens to you each day, and sometimes during the day. Therefore you may seek a partner who is independent, and who does not rely on you, and allows you space to wander off for an hour or so, without feeling rejected.

You may overanalyze your relationships, and constantly worry about what's not going right instead of appreciating the good parts. You may pick it to bits and look for every fault, which can be very destructive.

You enjoy parties but you are generally a private person. You love intimate meals with your partner where you can discuss your spirituality, or deep philosophical issues, or what you have materialized that day!

CAREER

With the 7 influencing your career you have the gift of bringing people together. You may become a recruitment officer, agent, or you may even be a professional 'matchmaker'! You would also excel as a 'New Age' healer, Feng Shui expert, psychologist, philosopher, or a producer (particularly documentaries).

You may also like to work on a nature reserve or in isolated parts of the world where there are not many people, for a while. Or, if you live in the middle of a great city you may work as a city analyst or become an administrator, researcher, photographer, chemist or surgeon. You may even like to indulge in your love of water and spend your whole life asail by joining the Navy.

When you are grounded and 'down to earth' you can materialize a small fortune with your strong mind and positive thoughts. When you are dreamy and living in the clouds of your imagination you may materialize little, and what you do earn may slip through your fingers, because you aren't 'earthed'.

With a 7, you have a strong intuition. When your funds are running low you will jump out of your mind and into your body and use your creative imagination and positive actions to help you to materialize your next pot of gold.

HOW YOUR PERSONALITY AND LIFE PATH WORK TOGETHER

If your Life Path Number is a 7, look below and match it up to your Personality Number; these two numbers offer the strongest and most important influences over your life. Read a few key points about how your Personality and Life Path Numbers work together.

7 LIFE PATH WITH A 1 PERSONALITY

With a 1 Personality and a 7 Life Path, you can learn to trust that you can achieve each goal, and that working on a goal will lead you eventually to your next goal. For example, you may be an inventor, and when you are working on a new invention you don't know if it will be successful. But working on it always leads you to your next invention, or your next goal. You need to trust (7) that your new inventions or ideas (1) will work, and if they don't, perhaps the next one will.

With a 7 Life Path you can learn to trust people so that you feel safe to care (1) and to get intimate with them. You can also learn to appreciate (7) and accept yourself (1) exactly as you are!

7 LIFE PATH WITH A 2 PERSONALITY

With a 7 Life Path and a 2 Personality you can learn to appreciate your ability to feel things so deeply, and you can also learn to trust your feelings or instincts. With a 7 influencing your Life Path you are also being asked to be honest and true to yourself about your feelings (2) so that you can be honest and truthful with others.

With a 2 influencing your Personality you love to share yourself and your life with your partner, friends, family and work mates. This is because you trust (7) people enough to 'let them in'. These people can teach you about their 'truths' (7), which can help you to find yours.

7 LIFE PATH WITH A 3 PERSONALITY

With a 7 influencing your life you can learn to appreciate your sense of humour (3) and your ability to uplift others and make them laugh (they surely appreciate you!).

With a 3 Personality you may experience confusion and inner conflict, and at times be unable to find any answers or truth (7) to the conflicts which arise in your life.

When you are scattered and your life is chaotic (3), trust (7) that life will work itself out, in its own time, and in its own way, to move you forward in the best possible direction.

7 LIFE PATH WITH A 4 PERSONALITY

With a 7 Life Path you like to be appreciated for your hard work and the effort (4) you put into life. When your efforts go unnoticed and you feel unappreciated (7) it can make you feel insecure (4). With a 4 you may be disloyal at times, and generally distrust (7) people.

With the 4 influencing your Personality you may persevere in finding out the truth (7) or your truth, within a situation. For example, someone may volunteer information about your work colleague which questions their behaviour. You would not take this on face value but ask your colleague directly to tell you their truth. Then you can work out in your own mind, your truth (7) about the situation, by finding out the facts.

7 LIFE PATH WITH A 5 PERSONALITY

With a 5 Personality you love adventure, and you love your freedom. With a 7 Life Path you can be encouraged to appreciate your freedom and not to take it for granted. When you feel free it usually means that you trust (7) life, and feel free (5) to follow its natural path and to 'go with the flow'.

With a 7 Life Path you may be distrustful of life and therefore procrastinate (5), or put off moving forward. For example, you may put off going for a job interview because you don't trust that you'll get the job. You may put off buying a new house because you don't trust the Estate Agent or the Surveyor. However, life has a habit of moving you forward even when you try your hardest to procrastinate and resist life.

7 LIFE PATH WITH A 6 PERSONALITY

With a 6 Personality you can learn to appreciate (7) your ability to nurture and care for yourself, and your ability to love and care for others. When you take yourself for granted (7) you can find that others fail to appreciate you too.

With a 6 Personality, you will be searching for your truth by working life out through the relationships you have. For example, with a 6 you may have many different partners, or commit yourself to one partner, for life. But these relationships can all teach you things, and help you to become 'whole' (6), and teach you the truth (7) about who you are.

7 LIFE PATH WITH A 7 PERSONALITY

With a 7 Personality and a 7 Life Path you are intensely influenced by the qualities of the 7. You may be very trusting (or too trusting and gullible at times), and you may have a deep sense of trusting your intuition. With two 7s influencing your life, you may crave solitude where you can contemplate your truth in peace. You may appreciate your sensitivity and your ability to be sensitive to others' needs.

You may also be very materialistic with the influence of both these numbers, and be too preoccupied with making money and producing things. Alternatively, you may live out your life from your living room and rarely travel further than your imagination.

7 LIFE PATH WITH AN 8 PERSONALITY

With your 7 Life Path you can really learn to appreciate your business flair (8), and appreciate your ability to follow your ambitions. With an 8 you may be stubborn and refuse to listen to common sense, or to trust (7) that you are on the 'right' path, when you are working towards your business goals.

With the influence of the 8 in your Personality you may reevaluate your life often, to try to find your truth. For instance, when you are mulling over a problem with your partner, you may reevaluate the situation daily to try to get to the bottom of it, and to find the truth within.

With an 8 you can be manipulative, and distrustful (7) of people at times, because they take you (and you may take them) for granted.

7 LIFE PATH WITH A 9 PERSONALITY

With a 7 influencing your Life Path you are learning to trust life, and your Personality is also teaching you (9) to do the same. When you trust in life you feel happier and relaxed because you know that whatever happens, it is for the best in the long run. When you trust yourself you can then be an example (9) and teach others to trust (7) life. Trust (7) that life will also teach you (9) the lessons you need to learn.

With a 9 Personality you can be extremely selfish and take everyone and everything for granted (7). With a 9 Personality you are also being taught to appreciate (7) and care about (9) everybody's needs.

HIGHLIGHTS OF NUMBER 7

POSITIVE	NEGATIVE
* Nature loving	* Gloomy
* Sensitive	* Overanalytical
* Trusting	* Distrustful
* Truthful	* Dishonest
* Realistic	* Dreamy

NUMBER 8

FAMOUS EIGHTS

Marlon Brando, Tatum O'Neil, Barbra Streisand, Shirley Bassey.

COUNTRIES

Argentina, Poland, China, Alaska, Papua New Guinea, Greenland.

GENERAL MEANINGS

Eight is the number for infinity, victory, karma and money.

PERSONALITY NUMBER 8

POSITIVE

With an 8 Personality you have enormous amounts of energy which you direct with your driving ambition towards your goals. You enjoy challenges because they give you an outlet for your energy and once you have mastered them, they can make you feel strong. You are assertive and like to stand up for your rights, in fact, nobody is going to walk all over you! You are very much in control, and like to think you know exactly where you are and what you are doing with your life.

You work extremely hard and with your business flair can make a great success out of whatever goals you attempt. This can, and often does, bring you recognition or even fame. You like to be the leading light or 'authority' in your chosen field; perhaps you know everything there is to know about beekeeping, music, law, etc.

With an 8 Personality you are a born organizer, and can organize your personal, social and work life with great expertise. You stride through life with force and direction, and you can certainly stand on your own two feet. At other times you can be passive, when you have exhausted yourself, for example. You can be quite a serious person, and you also take your responsibilities seriously. You like to reevaluate your life, and to take stock and weigh up other people and situations regularly – even on a daily basis. Then, if necessary, you can readjust your life accordingly.

You are practical, realistic and materialistic, and like to own or possess things. With an 8 you may have an abiding interest in money, fast cars and status, and have a strong sexual identity. You have no problems flaunting your body, wearing tattoos, expensive jewellery or designer clothes (perhaps with the label showing on the outside!). You are a smart dresser who likes to look neat, and you will usually look smart even when you are slouching around on lazy Sundays. You also like to look 'sexy' and may wear revealing clothes that highlight your strong identity. You like to give off an air of authority when you are walking down the street.

With your energy and drive you are a charming and magnetic person and you like to have similar people around you too. You may also be interested in spirituality which helps you to find inner happiness from the outer achievements in your life.

NEGATIVE

With the 8 influencing your Personality you are a stubborn person who at times likes to manipulate others and to get your own way. You are impatient; you want what you want, when you want it, otherwise forget it. You can be very hard on yourself and on others, and you put pressure on yourself to get things done. You are bossy, and you often tell others what you think is

best for them to do. You can be aggressive, argumentative and even a bully at times. You may like to dominate others, and you can even be ruthless, and try to gain a victory over them.

You may have an overinflated ego and, therefore, to you failure is a terrifying word, and one which you prefer to experience as little as possible. You may feel a failure even when things seem to be going well in your life. Failure to you usually means losing something you 'own'; you may lose your job, your relationship, or your home. Of course what you fail to remember is that once you have lost something, you then gain something else. For example, a new job, a new relationship or a new home. You are a fighter when it comes to your possessions, and you may knock people over when you are fighting for your goals.

With an 8 you crave authority, but you may also find challenges in dealing with anyone who is in authority, like your boss, a parent, a traffic warden, etc. You may be arrogant and flaunt your money, possessions, and even your partner in public, to boost your self-esteem and make you look good. Like an animal in a zoo you like to exhibit yourself and your worldly possessions, for all the world to see. You can have quite an attitude.

The 8 influencing your Personality gives you a great need for recognition, after all you are the only one who ever works so hard, and don't you deserve it! If you do succeed in becoming famous you can be unbearably proud. You can be arrogant and conceited, particularly when you do achieve your goals, and you like to boast about your achievements.

You can be an intense and 'heavy' person, and you may be rather grumpy at times. Sometimes you can be deadly serious about life, with little or no sense of humour, and you may take yourself deadly serious too.

With an 8 you can sometimes experience great frustration when you don't succeed within certain areas of your life. This lack of success can be because you bury yourself by being busy, and refuse to take stock of your life and look at what is happening around you.

You may also lack success because you are focusing too much on external things, and are not reevaluating your own behavior or what changes are going on inside you. For example, you may be so busy making money that you fail to notice a problem within your relationship. By stopping to reevaluate your life (even for an hour or a day), it can help you to examine the relationship. Then you can choose to continue with your life as it is, or to make adjustments to help improve the situation.

LIFE PATH NUMBER 8

POSITIVE

With an 8 Life Path you are learning to develop strength, to be an inspiration both to yourself and others, and to learn to handle power in a positive way.

NEGATIVE

With the 8 influencing your Life Path you can be weak at times, and lack inspiration, and you may feel powerless and unable to cope with life.

WISDOM NUMBER 8

POSITIVE

With the influence of the 8 in your Wisdom Number you have a practical gift of stamina, and can go on and on in pursuit of life.

NEGATIVE

Portraying the negative influences of the 8 in your Wisdom Number may mean you lack stamina or drive.

HOW THE NUMBER 8
INFLUENCES YOUR:

HEALTH

With an 8 you are generally physically strong and robust. However, you work hard at life, and can push yourself too far so that sometimes you become sick. Taking time off to rest isn't one of your favourite occupations and sometimes you may try to ignore health problems and carry on regardless. You may also dose yourself up with 'preparations' to help you cope, or perhaps you may try to vigorously work it out of your system at the gym (when you have a cold, for example). If you are bound to your bed – even for a day – you're likely to take your work with you, and have your telephone by your side.

You like to think you are in control of your body and your health, and so you may control what and how much you eat in order to help keep healthy. You can also be rigid with your diet and stick to the same menu, or the same routine, all the time. You take food seriously, and you probably know all the best restaurants in town, where you can eat exactly what you want.

For relaxation you may watch the ballet, gymnastics or motor racing, all of which display control and power which appeal to you. Generally you enjoy yoga, pilates, step classes, aerobics, jogging and riding.

RELATIONSHIPS

With an 8 you are highly magnetic, and you tend to attract to you strong, powerful people who have strong identities, and who are successful with their lives. Generally you require a partner to be able to 'stand on his or her own two feet' and to be financially independent. This is because you work hard to provide your own money, and you expect this from your partner too. However, you are happy to buy your partner presents, spend money on wonderful holidays together, and provide all the necessities in life. You may expect your partner to do the same for you too.

At home you may feel the need to constantly upgrade your television, computer, kitchen, car and to buy the best on the market. With an 8 you will generally want to find a partner who can contribute towards your status and authority, and make you feel secure.

With the 8 influencing your life you may be the strong, silent type, who can be quiet and passive and enjoy intimate dinner parties with your partner. Alternatively, you may be outgoing and aggressive at times, and enjoy loud parties and parading your partner around town. You may also be possessive, and want to dominate your partner, keeping him/her under your control.

You take your commitments seriously, so you don't jump into marriage or a long-term relationship without thinking it through very carefully. When you do decide to live with someone, or commit to them, it can help you to feel safe and secure.

CAREER

You may feel happiest in a career where you are in a position of power and authority, where you can use your organizational skills and take on lots of responsibility. You may also like to be in a position where you can empower others and help to bring out their strengths and help them improve their weaknesses. With an 8, you may prefer to work for a large organization, or you may own a (large) successful company yourself.

Money is an important issue with an 8, so a career as an accountant, or in a financial institution would be ideal. You may also make a good lawyer, librarian, administrator or secretary. You can help bring success to any company.

FINANCE

An 8 is strongly associated with money, so money is a major focus for you, and you like to have pots of it sitting in the bank. With your energy and driving ambition you can amply satisfy your needs, when you are prepared to work for them. Money gives you security and makes you feel powerful, and you can use it to acquire things which can then bring in more money. For example, stocks and shares, property, antiques and expensive jewellery.

HOW YOUR PERSONALITY AND LIFE PATH WORK TOGETHER

If your Life Path Number is an 8, look below and match it up to your Personality Number; these two numbers offer the strongest and most important influences over your life. Read a few key points about how your Personality and Life Path Numbers work together.

8 LIFE PATH WITH A 1 PERSONALITY

With an 8 Life Path you are learning to inspire people in a unique (1) way, and with your own individuality. With the 8 influencing your Life Path you can be inspired with new ideas, which can be expressed through your creativity (1). Your 8 Life Path can also inspire you to start (1) or pioneer new projects, and give you the inspiration to focus on them fully. Sometimes your new ideas may not inspire you at first, but when you start to focus (1) on them they spring to life. People may also be inspired (8) by your ability to focus on your goals, which can inspire them to do the same.

With a 1 Personality you may be withdrawn at times, and find it a challenge to accept, or step into your power (8), and into life. On the other hand, you may be a very powerful (8) individual who uses that power to focus (1) on your goals.

With a 2 Personality you are learning to co-operate and share your life with others. With an 8 Life Path you can develop the strength you need to co-operate with people. This can be in difficult situations when they are being defensive (2), and you are trying to co-operate with them. You can learn to listen to the other person's point of view (2), which can put you in a position of strength (8), because then you can see both sides.

With an 8, you may feel disempowered (8) by your indecisiveness (2). For example, two wonderful new jobs have been offered to you, and you simply cannot decide between the two. By not taking a decision you may lose both jobs and disempower yourself. Making decisions, especially important decisions, can make you feel powerful, because you know they are taking you further into life.

8 LIFE PATH WITH A 3 PERSONALITY

With an 8 Life Path and a 3 Personality you are able to inspire and uplift yourself during times of weakness (8) and confusion with your sense of humour (3). When others need the strength (8) to carry on you can also bring them joy (3), to help lighten their load.

You may feel powerless (8) when you become overwhelmed by the amount of chaos (3) in your life. With an 8 Life Path you can be inspired to sort out the 'mess' or the 'chaos' (3), so that you feel powerful and in control again. However, you may disempower yourself by refusing to sort out the mess (3), which may prevent you from getting on with your life.

8 LIFE PATH WITH A 4 PERSONALITY

With a 4 Personality you may like the security and stability of a regular job or a long-term relationship, but sometimes life just seems to plod on, with no real excitement in either. Your 8 Life

Path can inspire you, so that when things get too dull (4), you can breathe fresh air into your career, into your relationships, and into your life.

You can, with an 8 Life Path, feel uninspired when you find yourself getting too bogged down in routine (4). For example, every day you take the same journey to work, and you take the same bus or train. Day after day. You may feel so bogged down by the journey, that you may decide to leave your job just to change your (4) routine! Your 8 Life Path can help to inspire you to find new ways to travel to and from work, so that you can keep your job, and your security (4).

8 LIFE PATH WITH A 5 PERSONALITY

With a 5 Personality you have a lust for life and adventure, and you love to travel to all 'four corners' of the globe, which can inspire your 8 Life Path. Alternatively, the 8 in your Life Path can inspire you to travel, and to seek adventure (5), to feel fulfilled within your life.

With a 5 Personality you may be addicted to food, alcohol or drugs (caffeine for example), and you may at times feel powerless (8) to do anything about it. Your 8 Life Path can inspire you to look at why you think you need these addictions (5), and to help give you the strength (8) to face your life without them (if you choose).

8 LIFE PATH WITH A 6 PERSONALITY

With a 6 Personality you are a compassionate person who gives a great deal of love to your family and friends. With the influence of the 8 in your Life Path you can also be inspired to share this love with your community (6). You may do this by listening to your neighbour's problems, by being helpful to people, or professionally, as a doctor, nurse or community carer. Other people may be inspired (8) by your compassion (6) and it may encourage them to be compassionate too.

With an 8 Life Path you are inspired by beauty (6). You love beautiful fabrics, good food, colourful flowers, 'beautiful people', and you like to inspire yourself by wearing beautiful and sensual clothes. Perhaps you are a fashion designer (6) who designs powerful (8) and beautiful (6) clothes that inspire everyone who wears or sees them.

8 LIFE PATH WITH A 7 PERSONALITY

With an 8 influencing your Life Path you have the ability to inspire people (and yourself), with inner messages from your intuition (7), which can help give you guidance with your life. With a 7 you can be introspective and need time for solitude and rest; your 8 Life Path can help to empower you by allowing you this space.

With an 8 Life Path you may find that your strength (8) and your weakness (8) is your sensitivity (7). You may be over-sensitive at times, which is a weakness. You can also be insensitive to people, which is also a weakness. But at other times you are very sensitive (strength) and appreciate (7) others' needs.

8 LIFE PATH WITH AN 8 PERSONALITY

With an 8 Personality and an 8 Life Path this intensifies the influences from the 8. With two 8s influencing your life you may be a very strong, powerful person who delights in inspiring others with your ability to succeed. You are charming and attractive (magnetic). You can also be stubborn and proud, and manipulate others at times.

You work extremely hard, and often have the strength to carry through your ambitions and materialize your goals of power, status, and plenty of money! You may also develop your spirituality to help you balance your life, and to help you to find inner peace and happiness too.

8 LIFE PATH WITH A 9 PERSONALITY

With a 9 Personality you can be knowledgeable, and with an 8 Life Path you can be inspiring. You can also be inspired by the knowledge you acquire, and inspire others with your knowledge too. You may be a teacher, who inspires (8) others with the powerful (8) messages contained within your teaching.

With a 9 Personality you are highly critical of yourself and others; being critical is disempowering because it does not help you to move forward with your life. Instead, use your sharp intellect (9) and mind to think positively, so that you feel powerful and strong. Positive thoughts can inspire you and affect everyone around you in a positive way too.

HIGHLIGHTS OF NUMBER 8

POSITIVE	NEGATIVE
* Inspiring	* Lacking inspiration
* Strength	* Weakness
* Powerful	* Powerless
* Authoritarian	* Egotistic
* Success	* Failure

FAMOUS NINES

Mahatma Gandhi, Yoko Ono, Paul McCartney, Kevin Costner.

COUNTRIES

Syria, Ireland, Iraq.

GENERAL MEANINGS

Nine is the number for endings, new beginnings.

PERSONALITY NUMBER 9

POSITIVE

With a 9 Personality you have strong faith. You have faith in yourself, you have faith in others, and you have faith in life. Faith that life works itself out in its own way, and in a 'fair' way. You are a very 'fair' person, and you like to see 'fairness' done by everyone. You have a keen sense of judgement, but you do not express these judgements to hurt or infringe on the behaviour of others.

With the 9 influencing your Personality you also have your own definite beliefs about life; particularly on religious, political, social and environmental issues. You believe that everyone is entitled to the freedom to follow their own beliefs. Indeed you have a powerful intellect that likes to be stimulated by learning about issues concerning the whole world, because this helps to educate you.

You are a warm, open and friendly person who is very much interested in the welfare of others, which may be as important to you as your own. You are open to life and love to drink in knowledge from listening to people's points of view. You may be an academic who loves studying, and have your head in a book every day of your life. People think you are wise because you seem to know everything about anything, and you generally do! But it is also because you have an 'inner knowing' which comes from your psychic abilities and your strong instincts.

You have a strong mind that helps to balance out your emotions when you are feeling sensitive. You like to approve of others and you like others to approve of you. This is not because you are judging them but simply because you like to 'fit in' with everybody, and for people to like you. You can be conformist. With a 9 you are an optimistic person who is adaptable to change, and you do not get stuck in one point of view or belief. You are practical, with enormous amounts of common sense, and you have an ability to lead others to 'safety'.

You like to really understand yourself, and you are an understanding person. You have great respect for people and you believe in impersonality. That is, you generally do not take others 'personally', because you can understand why they do or say things, and respect and understand that they have their own beliefs.

You make a powerful teacher, and people are often inspired to follow the example you set, as a charitable human being.

NEGATIVE

With a 9 Personality you are judgemental and you constantly criticize others; this is particularly wearing on people who are close to you and is unhelpful and unproductive. You also criticize yourself; the way you look, and everything you do. You can be petty and pick on the smallest and most unimportant things, that really do not matter in the world at large.

You like to feel 'superior' and although you possess a fine wit, you can be highly sarcastic and unpleasant in your remarks at times. You are selfish; when you look at the world, you think, 'What can the world give me?' instead of 'What can I give the world?'

You may be very set in your beliefs and you may follow them almost with fanatical interest. You may join a religious, political or environmental group and get totally involved with their policies, or you may lead a campaign for them. You are happy to stand up for your beliefs.

Sometimes, with a 9, you can end up preaching at people rather than teaching them, even when you have good intent. This may be because of the intensity of emotion behind your beliefs, or your overemphasis on the morals concerned. You may also come across as a know-all and think you are the 'bee's knees'. With a 9 you may be challenged by other people's beliefs, but for you, they are either right or wrong, there is no in between. You also like to be right about things, and you can be ignorant to others' views.

With the 9 influencing your Personality you may also find you lack the courage of your convictions. You may suffer from a lack of belief or faith in yourself (and others), and you may remain non-committal when people ask you to give your point of view.

You may be constantly seeking approval from your partner, friends and family, and you may feel the need to 'obey' them. You may show a lack of understanding towards them when they are in difficult situations, and feel resentment and even bitterness towards helping them at times.

With a 9, you may try to 'take the law into your own hands' by inventing your own rules and regulations. For example, for your safety your gas boiler may need to be serviced once a year, on the advice of the manufacturer. However, you may decide to take no notice and set your own rule by saying you'll have it

serviced every two years. With a 9 you can be impractical at times, and lack common sense!

You can become regimental in your outlook and lead a regimented life, with everything running to precision timing.

With a 9 you can also be highly secretive and hold onto information that you hear, or knowledge that you gain, and use it for your own ends.

LIFE PATH NUMBER 9

POSITIVE

With a 9 Life Path you are learning to develop selflessness and to care for humanity and the world. Selflessness means 'not thinking of yourself' all the time and looking at the larger picture.

NEGATIVE

With the 9 influencing your Life Path you may be extremely selfish, with no interest in caring for people, and you may even be destructive towards the world in which you live.

WISDOM NUMBER 9

POSITIVE

With a 9 Wisdom Number your practical gift is the ability to discriminate about facts and life in a positive way. For example, being able to discriminate between whether to cross the road when there is no traffic, or to cross the road when there is traffic, is essential, and can prolong your life if you make the right judgement!

With a 9 influencing your Wisdom Number you may be unable to discriminate about life and situations, as you may be too emotional at times.

HOW THE NUMBER 9 INFLUENCES YOUR:

HEALTH

Generally, you are an open and relaxed person who takes life easy. You generally take good care of yourself. When you do get 'uptight' and tense, at times, it may be because you have been criticizing yourself too much, or judgemental about others, which can make your head ache.

When you are sick, and you are given a diagnosis from your doctor, you will either think it is 'right' or 'wrong' and may act accordingly. You don't like taking time off work, because you do not like to let others down.

However, when you do need to take to your bed, you certainly let everyone know! There you may entertain yourself (when not sleeping or watching current events on television) by reading spy stories or true romance novels.

With a 9 you are very sporty and you may enjoy competing in professional events. Swimming, tennis, rugby, football, polo … you enjoy most things. For relaxation and mental stimulation, you like to observe sporting games where you can use your discriminating mind to judge the winner. The Olympic Games was made for you, and if you don't attend them, then you enjoy staying plugged into your television (and video) for the whole grand event.

RELATIONSHIPS

With a 9 in a relationship you are idealistic and generally seek a partner with whom you can make a strong commitment. You are a moralistic person who may strongly believe in family values, and the marriage ritual. You are passionate and a true, loving romantic. You probably believe that romance can keep any relationship alive, or revive a dying one. This is despite your intellectual mind which can't quite believe you are romantic at all!

You like to be fair to your partner and there has to be give and take. For example, if your partner has been driving you to work for a whole week, then you think it's only fair to do the same the following week, or to do something else in exchange. Whatever you do you usually like to think you have your partner's approval, and you really need to feel loved. With a 9 influencing your life you can be quite critical at times, and judge your partner's every move.

With a 9 you are interested in religion; if you were born into a religious family you may think it is essential to marry or find someone with the same religious beliefs and outlook. However, as a 9 you are usually strong in your own beliefs. At the end of the day you may find a partner from your own religion, or from any religious background.

CAREER

With a 9 you may be interested in a career where you can help others. For example as a humanitarian, environmentalist, or doctor. You can excel as a teacher (particularly as a religious or spiritual teacher) by inspiring others with your beliefs and knowledge.

You may be an artist, musician, a great literary writer or academic, judge or diplomat. You can also be a leader in any field, and you may even enjoy working for the Secret Service, or anywhere which requires you to keep secrets.

With a 9 you are friendly and open to life, and when you are open you tend to attract money to you. You like saving your money for a rainy day because you are sensible. You are also as likely to give your money to charity or an environmental cause, as you are to give it to your family.

You enjoy good holidays when you need them, new clothes when you need them, and good food, but apart from that you may allow yourself few luxuries, even when you can easily afford them. However, on occasions, you can be self-indulgent too!

HOW YOUR PERSONALITY AND LIFE PATH WORK TOGETHER

If your Life Path Number is a 9, look below and match it up to your Personality Number; these two numbers offer the strongest and most important influences over your life. Read a few key points about how your Personality and Life Path Numbers work together.

9 LIFE PATH WITH A 1 PERSONALITY

With a 1 Personality you are a pioneer, and you can think up new ideas to help humanity to tackle its problems and challenges. With a 1 in your Personality you are also a problem solver, and you can use this gift to help solve problems for yourself and for the rest of the world too (9).

With your Personality influenced by a 1, you are very focused on your goals. Your 9 Life Path can help you to focus on goals that can help both you and humanity.

With a 9 Life Path you can be selfish, and you can be self-centred at times, and only interested in what the world (9) has to offer you. However, when you are selfish and self-centred

you may still be helping humanity. For example, you may be selfish by spending all your time on a new project at work (which will eventually benefit a lot of people), much to the regret of your partner, friends and family who do not see you for weeks on end.

9 LIFE PATH WITH A 2 PERSONALITY

With a 2 Personality you are placid, and when people in your environment (9) are stressed, you can help them by listening (2) to their problems, and caring for them. Your 9 Life Path can also help you to be selfless (or caring) towards yourself, on days when you may be feeling vulnerable (2) and unable to cope with life.

Your 2 Personality can encourage you to co-operate (2) with your environment (9). Your environment is the world you live, work, play and sleep in, and the people in your life, as well as the air you breathe and the water you drink. You also have your inner environment. By co-operating and sharing with people you are also helping your environment.

9 LIFE PATH WITH A 3 PERSONALITY

With a 3 Personality you have an 'happy-go-lucky' nature. You can help humanity (9) by caring for your social environment with your energy and enthusiasm, and with your ability to spread a little light in people's lives. At times you may be scattered (3) and you may need to get selfish (9) in order to draw in your energies and recharge your batteries, by refraining from helping others.

With a 3 Personality and a 9 Life Path you may be very interested in religion and the spiritual values within society. These values may help you to lead a happier life, which can then feed your social environment (9); your home, your workplace and everywhere you go.

9 LIFE PATH WITH A 4 PERSONALITY

With a 4 Personality you may be concerned with your physical welfare or your physical survival because you can feel insecure. Your 9 Life Path can help you by teaching you to be selfless and not to get overly concerned about the world having to provide security (4) for you. When your 9 positively influences your Personality you can selflessly help others to survive. For example, by offering them shelter, feeding them, giving them work, and by offering them security in whatever way you can.

You may, with a 4 Personality, work consistently to help others in a selfless way (9). Alternatively, you may be lazy (4) and fail to put any effort into supporting your environment and humanity.

9 LIFE PATH WITH A 5 PERSONALITY

With a 5 Personality you can learn to be adaptable to changes (5) within your environment (9). This may be adapting to little changes in your life, like moving to a different office at work. You can also learn to be adaptable to larger changes, like moving house, or a change in government within your country. With a 5 Personality you can help others (9), or humanity, to adapt to changes in their lives.

With a 5 influencing your Personality you have an inquiring mind, and you like to know (9) scientific facts about the world you live in. For example, you will like to know about the rainforests, medicine, health and social issues, global warming, etc. With selflessness, you can then see how you can help humanity. With a (9), you can be a selfish person; you may prefer to know how all these changes are going to affect your life and you!

9 LIFE PATH WITH A 6 PERSONALITY

Caring for humanity also means caring for yourself – because you are a part of humanity. With a 6 Personality you love to

nurture and care for yourself, and you also have the ability to be deeply compassionate and caring towards others too. This also includes caring for your partner, your family, friends, work colleagues, and anybody you come into contact with in your daily life. You can be selfish and not see the needs of your community, only your own at times.

With the 6 influencing your Personality you have an appreciation of beauty, and you appreciate the beauty within your environment (9) and within the human race.

9 LIFE PATH WITH A 7 PERSONALITY

With a 7 Personality you are a sensitive person and are very aware of your environment (9). You are philosophical and you think and care deeply about the needs of humanity. With a 7, you are also an instigator, and when applying this in a selfless (9) way, you can help to make things happen to improve conditions in the world.

With a 9 Life Path you can be uncaring and cold (7) towards others, and selfish in your desire to evade your own or others' problems, by becoming too introspective and dreamy. Alternatively, you may use your imagination (7) to think up practical ways in which you can help yourself and your environment.

9 LIFE PATH WITH AN 8 PERSONALITY

With an 8 Personality you are an initiator, who can initiate projects and ideas to help yourself, your environment (9), and the world you live in. You are a practical person (8) and may like to help humanity in a practical way. For example, by giving blood once a year, or by raising money and collecting material things for world causes.

With an 8 influencing your Personality you can develop your strength, during times of need, or when you seem to be failing in life. With an 8 you can also be a tower of strength to people

within your environment (9). You can also be stubborn (8) and selfish (9) and only see how the world can make you richer and more successful (8).

9 LIFE PATH WITH A 9 PERSONALITY

With a 9 Life Path and a 9 Personality, you are influenced intensely by the number 9. With a 9 you are a humanitarian and perhaps you are a leader in the field of religion, politics or medicine, or you are extremely artistic and musical.

You may be very friendly, open and warm so that others listen to your opinions and beliefs when you are teaching, or leading them. You can be very caring, loving and selfless towards your family and your community. At other times you can be very selfish, critical, and preach your own morals at people, and feel put out when they don't accept your points of view.

HIGHLIGHTS OF NUMBER 9

POSITIVE	NEGATIVE
* Selfless	* Selfish
* Unconditional love	* Resentful
* Fair	* Critical
* Open	* Secretive
* Discriminative	* Judgemental

NUMEROLOGY EXPERIENCES

There are many reasons why you may be interested in experiencing Numerology and there are many different ways by which you may go about this. You can have a personal reading from a Numerologist, you can have a chart reading from a shop that offers Numerology computer analysis, or you can take part in a group workshop or course. You can even find accurate inspirational material about your chart on the Internet or you can learn from books (like right here!)

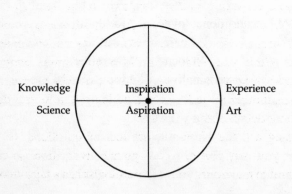

Numerologists work out your chart using varying methods depending upon their different schools of thought. However, when you arrange to have a professional reading they will certainly take your date of birth and usually your full birth names (on your birth certificate). Most Numerologists additionally work out your yearly influence number, and your age, because these numbers highlight the kind of issues, circumstances and events that can affect you during that year. This is particularly relevant if you are needing to focus on one specific problem, to find out how old you were when it started, what you were learning that year, and its potential for change.

You may be visiting the Numerologist because you have a health, career, or relationship problem, and may simply like to focus on one of these specific areas, or on your goals in life. However, a Numerologist usually gives you a general reading with the overall feel to your chart before you focus on specific problems. This can help you to understand your basic patterns of behaviour, your strengths and weaknesses, and your potential. A general reading usually lasts around one hour.

The Numerologist can go into great depth about your life, and can focus on the physical, emotional, mental and spiritual elements within your chart. That is, on your mind, body and spirit. In addition to the numbers one to nine they may also use any other number up to 81 (which adds up to a 9) in order to obtain finer details about your life.

You may ask the Numerologist lots of questions, or take notes, or you may like to record your conversation, so check beforehand to make sure your Numerologist has a tape recorder (most do).

Visiting a Numerologist with your partner, either because you are experiencing problems within your relationship, or to

look at your potential together is also common. Again most Numerologists will highlight key points about your individual charts before discussing your compatibility.

Sometimes you may like to know more information about a partner whom you have just met, but the Numerologist can only give you very superficial details without them being present (without their permission). Numerology can also help you to review old relationships which may be preventing you from moving forward.

You may prefer to have a personal reading rather than work in a group setting because it offers you privacy. Visiting a Numerologist is fun and fascinating and most people are surprised by the accuracy of the information revealed by the simple digits one to nine!

VISITING A NUMEROLOGIST FOR A BUSINESS READING

In order to prepare a company chart for yourself and/or your business partners you will need to supply your company registration date, and its registration number. If you did not register your company then the actual day you started trading can be used as its birth date. The Numerologist also needs to know your personal birth date if you own the company, and any business partners' dates, because these have a strong influence over the company, too.

Numerology can also help you to potentially find the best time to commence trading, to find a suitable name, when to launch products, and also with recruitment too.

If you are unable to make a personal visit, you can obtain a postal reading on cassette from many Numerologists. For this you will need to send your date of birth and names, along with any questions about areas you would like to focus on, or simply request a general reading. The Numerologist will then send you a personal tape.

The advantage of this method of Numerology is that you can play your tape anytime, and there is no need for you to miss out on an opportunity because the Numerologist does not live nearby. You may also ask the Numerologist for a tape for a friend's birthday present, which can be posted on to them.

HOW OFTEN DO I NEED TO SEE A NUMEROLOGIST?

You can have a very general Numerology reading or go into great depth about your life, for as long as you are interested in working on your personal development. Therefore you may only need one reading, or you may take time to assimilate the information, and go back later to find out more. Some people may visit a Numerologist many times over a short period, or once a year for life … whatever you need.

CHILDREN'S VISITS TO A NUMEROLOGIST

Children are particularly receptive or 'open' to Numerology and thoroughly enjoy having their chart read. You may take your child to a Numerologist because he or she is having problems at school, behavioural problems at home, or even health problems. Working with Numerology can help you and them to

discover root causes of their problems, even in their relationship to you, as a parent, if you feel this is appropriate. Alternatively, you may like to understand a little about your child's potential, and by highlighting their gifts it can help them to make useful and important decisions about their life.

GROUP WORKSHOPS

Numerology helps you to develop your intuition and there is no better way to do this than with a group of like-minded people who are all there to learn with the same focus in mind. Group work is challenging, because sometimes it requires you to share yourself with someone else or with the whole group (if you choose). It is also rewarding because learning about others means you are learning more about yourself, and it is assisting your personal development, and expanding your experiences and your knowledge about life. Working within a group is always more powerful than working alone because the group dynamic can be very powerful.

During a group workshop you will be requested to keep confidentiality about other participants. This is important because it enables you to feel safe to share with others and to respect people's personal identities and their experiences.

The benefits you can expect from a group workshop are your interaction with others, personal development from working on your own chart, and the development of your intuition by practising Numerology. Participating in a group workshop can also inspire you to go on to take professional training in Numerology, and give you a tool to take home and share with others. You can learn about your family by bringing awareness to their strengths and weaknesses, learn more about your gifts, learn about your patterns within relationships, which can then help you to heal yourself and relate to others.

Some schools offer formal qualifications in Numerology but a good way to find out about a teacher and a school is through personal recommendation. Many Numerologists teach students for many years and never advertise their classes because they are always full. Other Numerologists advertise in your local New Age magazines or in wholefood shops or book shops.

Methods taught to Numerology students can vary greatly. What is certain is that when you enrol for a course in Numerology you most certainly will learn about the qualities of the numbers 1 to 9 from your date of birth, about your names, and more about yourself and life in general. After completing a professional Numerology course you may decide to take it up as a career and use Numerology to help others, or add it to your current career so that you continue to work with this fascinating subject.

THE INTERNET

There is a tremendous amount of fascinating information from around the world on Numerology on the Internet. Everything from general history to how to find out about your own birth chart. For this you will need your own computer or to visit a web site at an Internet store or cafe. The benefit of this is that you can tune in any time (at home) and the information on it is continually being updated.

NUMEROLOGY FOR EVERYONE

Numerology can help everyone, and whichever method you experience it by, and by whatever means (personal reading, workshop, etc) it can help you to grow and enrich your life.

CURRENT INTEREST

Numerology has gained enormous popularity around the world, particularly as a result of the lottery. Lotteries are held in many countries, including Australia, America and the United Kingdom. They have brought numbers to the forefront – numbers are a talking point – with many people using their date of birth as their personal lottery numbers in each competition.

Numbers are used more and more in advertising on the television, in magazines and on the street. Magazines also print regular Numerology pages, similar to those used in Astrology, to highlight health, relationships and career. These are fascinating and enable readers to get a glimpse of their potential.

Access to the Internet means you are able to tune into endless amounts of information from around the world on the Numerology Sites. With some Numerology sites you can tap in your date of birth and it will instantly display a daily, weekly or annual chart for you. You can go for superficial information on the Net right through to the deeper philosophical side of Numerology. The Internet is easily accessible for many people, and definitely adds to the escalating interest in Numerology.

Workshops and courses are now available all over the world and these inspire people to practise Numerology with their friends, family and as a profession.

NUMEROLOGY
AND BEYOND

Now you have read this book you know a little more about numbers, and that they are not simply black and white calculations on a page but are energies that spring to life with hidden messages, meanings and influences. Potent numbers that can reveal strengths, weaknesses and potential within the cycles they represent.

WHAT HAVE YOU LEARNED?

In this book you have learned how to use Numerology to find out more about your health, your relationships, your career and your finances – all from your birth date. Your names and age have also been calculated to give you additional information about the trends or influences over the kinds of experiences you may have in your life.

Numerology can be applied to advertising, features in newspapers, politics, religion, economics, the weather, indeed anything in life, to help you understand what is truly being communicated and understood.

LEARNING BY MEMORY

It can help you to memorize some of the basic qualities of the numbers 1 to 9, and the A–Z chart on page 5, because you can add things up in your head as you go along. For example, if somebody asks you to arrange a date for an important meeting, you can remember the qualities of that date and see if it 'jumps out at you'. By feeling really good about the date you have arranged for your appointment, it can boost your confidence and help you get the most out of it. This also applies to dates with intimate partners, for travel, for business deals, and so on. However, ideally it is up to you to make the most out of each day, no matter whether it 'feels right' or not, and to make the most out of your life.

WHERE DO YOU GO FROM HERE?

You may be a little wiser after reading this book as you now know a little more about Numerology. However, even when you have read it once you can still read it again. Have you ever re-read a book and thought, 'I don't remember this being in it before'? This is because you usually take in only a percentage of the information at once, and each time you read something again, you discover new things. Perhaps you originally read the book at home, or on your way to work. Maybe you have moved job or house since you last read it, and your perspective has changed. Therefore, the way you will understand Numerology may have changed too.

If you have read this book and are interested in visiting a Numerologist, or taking a workshop or course then look at the next section, 'Professional Contacts', to see how you can go about this.

PROFESSIONAL CONTACTS

HOW TO FIND A NUMEROLOGIST

As Numerology is a fast-growing industry, there are many individuals and schools around the world, not on this list. They often advertise in health food shops, complementary health centres, bookshops, or in your local press. However, personal recommendation is often best.

Below is a list of professional organizations whom you can contact too. You can find out about professional training and workshops, or find out how you can go about having a personal or business reading with a professional Numerologist. Please also send a stamped addressed envelope or International Reply Coupon.

AUSTRALIA

Character Analysis and Numerology
Mrs C Anschutz
23 Flinders Street
Kent Town
5067
S. Australia

FRANCE

Christian Gilles School
Residence de L'Abbey Royale
17 Rue Pirel
93200 Saint Denis
PARIS

NEW ZEALAND

Francie Williams
North Shore Parapsychology School
60 East Coast Bay Road
Milford
00649 4101182

UNITED KINGDOM

Association Internationale de Numerologues (A.I.N.)
PO Box 867
Harrow
Middlesex
HA1 3XL

Connaissance School of Numerology
Royston Cave Art and Bookshop
8 Melbourne Street
Royston
Hertfordshire
SG8 7BZ

UNITED STATES

Marina D Graham
7266 Bennett Valley Road
Santa Rosa
CA 95404-9738